MW00615862

# Life on the Sunny Side

# Life on the Sunny Side

INSPIRATIONS FOR BUSY WOMEN
THAT WILL IGNITE YOUR DREAMS
AND BRIGHTEN YOUR LIFE

*Sunny Simon*

Copyright © 2020 Sunny Simon
Published in the United States by: Raise the Bar High Books

All rights reserved. This book or any portion thereof may not be reproduced
by any mechanical, photographic or electronic process or in the form of
a phonographic recording; nor may it be stored in any retrieval system,
transmitted, or otherwise copied for public or private use – other than for
"fair use" brief quotations embodied in the articles and reviews except as
permitted under Sections 107 or 108 of the United States Copyright Act
without prior written permission of the publisher.

The author of this book does not dispense medical advice or prescribe
the use of any technique as a form of treatment for physical, emotional or
medical problems without the advice of a physician. The intent of the author
is only to offer information of a general nature to help create a positive life
style.

To protect the privacy of others, certain names and details have been
changed.

Cover design: Durski
Copyediting: Tracie Schatz

# Dedication

*To My Nieces*
*May you always walk on the sunny side*
*To My Forever Friends*
*You are my sunshine tribe, my teachers*

***In Memoriam***
*To My Mother*
*My master teacher who taught me to live on the sunny side*

## What Reader's Are Saying About *Life on the Sunny Side*

I love this book! It's a beautifully written gem for us gals on the run. I downloaded it on my phone to read a story or two when I have a few minutes. I really appreciate that Sunny does not waste words. In her no-nonsense style, she quickly takes you to the heart of the issue and peppers you with takeaways you can put into immediate action. I found some great stories I can use, for examples, in my speeches on earning loyalty for both private and corporate environments. Sunny's glass-half-full perspective will inspire you to face down fear, fight negativity, and become a change agent!

**Irma Parone**
Parone Group,
International Best Selling Author - *Voices of The 21ˢᵗ Century*

Sunny Simon consistently delivers feel good takeaways that help you create your best life. Every time I picked up *Life on the Sunny Side* I felt comforted after reading these timely vignettes. Five minutes is all you need to feel better about your life with Sunny's words that motivate you to take action.

**Ellen Paris**
Contributor, Forbes.com

Oh My Goodness, I got so excited when I started reading this book; it was just what I had been seeking. *Life on the Sunny Side* is a problem-solving book that comes with personal anecdotes and heartfelt solutions for any problem you encounter and want to improve upon. You'll find the motivation to keep you going.

Let's face it; we all have something we need to work on. No one is perfect, and no one has to be, but the book will give you all you need to be that ideal woman, or at least a woman content with who she is, a woman with big feelings and big dreams to reach a higher self. You are a woman who can set goals and learn how to stick with them. You have lots of girlfriends to keep on, keeping on, and now you have Sunny to lead the way. She probably hears it all the time, but my advice is "Put a little Sunny in your life," and you won't be sorry for it.

I like how you can go to whatever chapter catches your attention, "the something" you know you need to work on. Then the next day, go back and read chapter one if you want. Read it cover to cover or skip around, whatever works. There is something in the book for everyone. I think you will be just like me, you will want a copy for your daughter, one for your niece, one for your bestie, and whomever else, but you will not want to give your copy away. You will definitely want to hold on to it, as you'll want to go back to it over and over to keep the motivation going. A lovely read, a simplistic and heartfelt advice book with all the positive feels. Have fun with your read, I sure did!

**Carolyn Barry**
American Business Women's Association
Top Ten Business Woman

What a wonderful book filled with positive messages for everyone! Sunny Simon is a master at understanding the human condition. In our modern world, women are expected to keep up, reach higher, go faster and farther, while looking beautiful, raising kids and keeping the home running smoothly. With so much on our plate, there's bound to be a few things that suffer.

This book is filled with sweet vignettes and parallels helping us choose our way from dark to light. There are factual references and important lessons shared within these pages that are sure to help each one of us find peace, love and boundless joy.

**Eve Gaal**
Eve holds a Master's Degree in Human Behavior and a Bachelor's in English Literature. She is the author of *The Happy War, Penniless Hearts, Penniless Souls* and a short novella, *The Fifth Commandment.* Her work has appeared in The Los Angeles Times, The Daily Pilot, several anthologies and online. More about her at www.evegaal.com

# Foreword

Sunny Simon has given the world an incredible book, *Life on the Sunny Side*. It is a must-read for anyone, man or woman, young or old. She sets out in black and white, a life path, with wonderful vignettes to hone in on the lesson she is offering. Whether it is personal organization for cultivating essential habits, or dealing with procrastination, Simon's words will have you hooked on its common-sense for happy everyday living, even if you are detoured by a bump or two in the road. *Life on the Sunny Side* will teach you how to grow despite adversity. Her words will help you meet the challenges of everyday life.

Simon is no stranger to adversity. The words she writes are not just platitudes, but a thoughtful compilation of various situations and solutions she has experienced. After many years in the corporate world, Sunny discovered a position in corporate management wasn't fulfilling her dreams and ambitions. With all the skills she had learned plus her first-hand knowledge, she transformed her life to become a life and career coach. Her resume writing and negotiation skills are without peer.

The stories in *Life on the Sunny Side* will give you lots of laughter and maybe a few tears as you turn the pages. It should also provide ideas about your future. Whatever life cycle you find yourself in, read this book. I know you will find your life enriched. Mine was.

Judith Fabris
Author of *Sargent's Lady, The Missing Driscoll, Kameleona, Money Cool*

# About This Book

I'LL KEEP THIS BRIEF. *LIFE on the Sunny Side* is a book of life lessons accumulated and penned during my corporate and entrepreneurial career. Some have been published in newspapers, blogs, and newsletters. Hats off to my clients, friends, family, and all the incredible individuals I've encountered along the way who left their mark on me. You'll read a few tales about my nieces Aisalynn and Alina, because I have found that children are often our best teachers.

Each chapter contains a series of the two minutes reads I promised you on the back cover. These stories provide suggested takeaways for making positive changes in your life. Read it in bite-sized time slots, or in one sit-down session, whatever suits your lifestyle.

I know you're busy, so I'll leave you with these parting words: My wish is that you will find inspiration within these pages to power-up your day and brighten your life.

# Table of Contents

# Inspiration
# Influential Motivation

"What you lack in talent can be made up with
desire, hustle and giving 110% all the time.

— DON ZIMMER

# Life Lessons from The Coach

RECENTLY I LEARNED THE LATE beloved college basketball coach, John Wooden, carried around a treasured gift from his father. On a tattered and aged piece of paper was the creed on which he based his life. I was in awe. I had to find out more about this Midwestern man touted as being "College basketball's most successful coach" and named by ESPN "Coach of the Century."

This amazing legend grew up on an Indiana farm. His childhood home had no electricity or indoor plumbing. As a high school basketball hero, he led the home team to three consecutive finals. He married a lovely lady who played cornet in the school band. They were married for 53 years, separated only by death.

Okay, maybe you knew all that, but I didn't. Wooden's "life list," the creed his father bestowed upon him, consists of seven simple sentences: "Be true to yourself. Make each day a masterpiece. Help others. Drink deeply from good books, especially the Bible. Make friendship a fine art. Build a shelter for a rainy day. Pray for guidance, count, and give thanks for your blessings every day."

I now understand how this legendary coach could bring out the best in his players. He was authentic in a world where truly genuine human beings are rare. He role modeled wisdom, kindness, integrity, and love. I also understand he had a sage father who created a treasure map for his son. Somehow I think that trumps assets in a will. Those life lessons are filled with something more satisfying than wealth.

Wooden co-authored a book, *My Personal Best: Life Lessons from an All-American Journey.* I want him to coach me, so I'm going to read it. But in the meantime, I've decided to create my life list. I'll borrow some belonging to the coach and add things I need to work on like: Give love completely without keeping score and practice patience daily.

How about you? Would now be a good time to create a life list? I think no matter what stage of life you're in; it's never too late to chart a course for the rest of your days on this planet. Invest some time in it this week. As Coach Wooden would remind us, "Never cease trying to be the best you can be. That's in your power."

# Be That Person

RECENTLY I READ THIS POST on Facebook: "Be the person your dog thinks you are." I smiled because my dog thinks I'm pretty special. I know because he follows me wherever I go, spends hours beside me at my desk, and shows immense gratitude when a dog cookie appears. But I have a bit of a spin on that sentiment. My thought is: "Be the person you wish you knew." I'm talking about the one you could have used in your life to make things just a bit easier.

I lost my mother in my early twenties. Sure, I survived as a motherless young adult; however, I yearned for a wise aunt. Someone I could turn to for some mature sage advice, someone who knew my mother, someone to share the loss, the tears, triumphs, and someone to watch me walk down the aisle.

Who was that missing person in your life? Maybe one of the cool kids who would have invited you to sit at that coveted lunch table and helped you feel comfortable? Perhaps a wise mentor to show you the ropes when you got your first job? What if you had a teacher who encouraged and showed an interest in you? A coach who believed in you? Maybe it was a parent who was missing from your life.

As luck would have it, I am fortunate enough to have nieces providing me with the opportunity to perform the role missing in my life. Think about it. What person needs you in his or her life?

When you find that individual, make a difference, be a helping hand, and hold a hand when needed. Listen with both your head and your heart. Lend a shoulder to cry on, and then speak your truth. Never withhold a dose of tough love if that is the required remedy. As Aristotle advised, "Lead from your heart and mind and listen to theirs." Do these things, and you will be a positive story in someone else's life.

This week I invite you to spend some time identifying that person absent from your life. Know that you are the missing link in the presence of a friend, a child, or at this point, a mere stranger. Pursue and build a relationship and let your stardust rub off on that individual. I promise you; it will be fulfilling. Someone out there needs you, your talents, and your superpowers. Be the person you wish you knew.

# The Candle and the Mirror

MOST PEOPLE HAVE A SUPERHERO or a robust role model. Who is the person you look up to and admire? For me, it's Carol. When I met her over 20 years ago, I decided to be like her when I grew up. My dilemma is I don't think I'll ever catch up. Although I keep evolving, she is still light years ahead of me.

What's so special about Carol? In addition to being the most positive person I know, she is incredibly resilient. Although I suspect she is not perfect, I am at a loss to identify her human flaws. She is "Carol the Wonder Woman" as my group of friends affectionately dubbed her.

The other day, she did a back summersault flip off her patio (a purely freak accidental happening) and sustained some severe damage to her body. She is now safely out of the woods and in a rehab center. When I called her to check in, Carol sounded cheerful, as if she were sipping cocktails on the beach in Malibu rather than drinking watered-down hospital beef broth. She views her rehabilitation as a fascinating learning experience. No doubt, when she is released, the staff will present her with a Miss Congeniality trophy as they say tearful good-byes. She is the kind of person you want to hang with, hoping her admirable qualities will rub off and cling to you.

Here's the thing about bonding with positive people. They do make you better. When I first met Carol, we worked in the HR department of a telecommunications company. I studied her as if she were a science project. Each morning I watched her step through the office threshold and beam her dazzling smile at everyone she encountered. She reminded me of the Edith Wharton quote: "There are two ways of spreading light: to be the candle or the mirror." Somehow, she is both.

Carol's office was a revolving door. Managers sought her out for advice and counsel. Observing them leave, I could sense their burdens lifting. For two years, I watched, learned, and became a better version of myself.

So who are you hanging out with these days? Is there a Carol in your life? If the answer is yes, continue to kindle the relationship. Need a positive role model? Be optimistic. Send out bright vibes and extend your love outward. The positive energy you create will attract precisely the kind of person you want as a role model.

# Earning Your Superstar Stripes

ONE OF MY FAVORITE CLIENTS is someone I categorize as a superstar. It's easy to describe her secret to success. She pushes through her fear. Upon setting a goal, this young professional pursues it with careful thought and with enthusiasm. She is a small business owner with a broad vision. Although I am confident this smart lady has a lofty IQ, she knows she cannot do it all and taps into the appropriate mentors and experts to help her reach the goal line.

I met Dominique several years ago at a businesswomen's group. She just completed a major relocation across the country. Despite the transition phase, she seemed so grounded. Her strategy is forward-thinking. Dom researched the group months before her move and began making inroads to members online. Upon landing in the Coachella Valley, she already had established a network of friends and potential clients for her fledgling business.

If no one has ever labeled you a superstar (except your mother), you can earn that title by making a few changes. Begin by pulling out your annual goals for a quick review. Are your objectives large enough to force you out of your comfort zone? If not, revisions are necessary.

Now, test your vision. If you are preparing for a future career move, spend a moment looking beyond the target. What will you strive for once you achieve that goal? You can enlarge your vision by challenging yourself to push the boundaries. For example, if you are a first-line supervisor vying for a move up the management ladder, a logical step would be directing a more extensive staff. Now that you have defined the next position, map out what you need to do to get there.

Steps on the way to superstar status are scary. Don't allow fear to veer you away from risk. Do you believe you are ready for a promotion? Ask for it! The worst thing that could happen is getting a firm no. Rebound from the negative answer by asking what actions need addressing before you reach the next level. Knowing what to do puts you one step closer to your goal.

Reaching superstar level means putting yourself out there. People like Dominique subscribe to Woody Allen's philosophy. "Eighty percent of success is just showing up." Anyone who knows my client will agree, she always shows up, stays in the moment, and adds value.

Life begins when you step outside your comfort zone. Keep pushing those boundaries, and you will succeed. Herb Kelleher, the former CEO of Southwest Airlines, put it this way: "We have an action plan, it's called doing things."

Challenge yourself to action. Superstardom is within your reach. Just keep showing up and continue reaching for the stars.

# Letter to Self

WHILE SCROLLING THROUGH FACEBOOK, I paused on the following letter to self: "Don't get worked up over things you cannot change, people you cannot change. It's not worth the anger build up or the headaches. Instead, control what you can. Everything else let go."

That's excellent advice, but what made me take a long look at the post was the concept of self-coaching. Granted, we all know how to follow through on goals, do the right thing, and listen to our wise inner voice, but why don't we? I can answer that one with a multitude of reasons; fear of failure, fear of success, laziness, aversion to change, and the list goes on.

Let's step back for a moment and instead of writing up a list of resolutions for a new year, how about writing a note to self. In the book, *Be Your Own Life Coach*, author Fiona Harrold advises we look inside ourselves rather than outside for solutions, assurance, and guidance. So let's do that. Here's your assignment. Spend the next 30 minutes scanning last year in your mind's eye. What did you do well, and why? What could you have done better? Do a deep dive to discover the core reason you failed on goals. Your objective is to gain clarity and develop the confidence to accept your own advice.

For example, maybe you failed at losing weight and becoming more physically fit. Could the reason be you hate going to the gym because you find it boring and mundane? Perhaps you'd rather go dancing. Well, that's it! Advise yourself to throw all your energy into dancing. Take lessons in all forms of dance (money should not be an issue; if you cannot afford it, go to YouTube) dance daily and set your sights on entering a dance competition. Get the picture?

Perhaps you need a role model. I have one. A very techy friend of mine just dropped 50 pounds utilizing virtual reality exercise. She loves technology and told me it was the most fun she ever had exercising. Guided by intuition and self-coaching, she found the perfect match.

Now that you have examined your shortfalls, you are wiser. Your next action item is to take on the role of coach and recommend specific actions by writing an inspiring letter to yourself. Most importantly, do it tenderly. I love a section written by novelist Brenna Clarke in the book *What I Know Now: Letters to My Younger Self.* She writes, "Brenna honey, try more things. Cross some lines. You should be cooking on all four burners."

Wisdom is a result of your mistakes and failures. Use that to your advantage. Work on being your own best friend and coach yourself to success. Be bold, and be brilliant!

# Just Think About It

I'VE ALWAYS CONSIDERED MY CAR an educational institution. While commuting any distance, I plug into something motivational or enlightening to expand my knowledge base. Recently on a drive, I listened to an interview with self-made billionaire, Sara Blakely, founder of SPANX women's shape-wear. I had to smile when she described the use of her vehicle.

Sara has a five-minute commute from home to the Spanx headquarters but spends 45 minutes driving aimlessly around Atlanta before arriving at her office. Why? Her car is her think tank. She describes thinking as one of her favorite hobbies. Driving around provides the opportunity to let her mind wander. Compulsive about capturing creative thoughts, Sara never leaves home without her trusty spiral-bound Mead notebook.

What works best for Sara is her car; however, accomplishing some heavy-duty creative thinking can be done anywhere. While some prefer a solitary walk in a quiet setting to brainstorm, others like an environment with background noise. According to a study performed by researchers at the University of Illinois at Urbana-Champaign, 70 decibels is an ideal setting for percolating out-of-the-box ideas, explaining why many individuals enjoy working at coffee shops.

Besides the background noise factor, birthing creative ideas has something to do with your body clock. Although it may seem counterintuitive, there is a school of thought professing your brain works better when you are fatigued. For some individuals, a tired brain lacks a singular focus and tends to wander, which is often ideal for abstract thinking.

Another way to garner those eureka moments is exercise, explaining why many people like to go for an invigorating run. Albert Einstein claims the theory of relativity came to him while riding his bike.

On the flip side, try dreaming your way into creative ideas. That worked for Keith Richards, who credits sleeping for part of the song "Satisfaction," the smash hit released in 1965 by the Rolling Stones.

Whatever your modus operandi, it pays to awaken your creative juices. Doing so can help you discover the answer to a nagging problem or set the stage for a brilliant new product idea, as was the case for SPANX entrepreneur Sara Blakely.

Get introspective. Whether it's fresh air and a brisk walk to erase those cobwebs from your mind, or perhaps you do your best thinking in the shower or while enjoying a power nap. Whatever the case, find that sweet spot and engage your creative spirit.

# How My Dog Made Me a Better Person

ZOLTON IS MY SEVEN-YEAR-OLD SHIH Tzu. He has an uncanny way of becoming my teacher. I work out of my home office. Although I am present in the room, I may not be present in his life. Yes, I take the time to scratch him behind the ears when he shows up at my desk, and then I quickly bribe him with cookies so I can return to work. I tell myself I am far too busy to spend time with my dog.

One morning Zolton dog taught me I was not "walking the talk." I preach to all my clients the value of quiet time, insisting they spend a few minutes in nature or just sitting in silence daily. Turning down the noise to reflect, think, get creative, and make sound decisions is essential to healthy living. On that day, Zolton was incredibly persistent in vying for my attention. He refused to be tempted into oblivion by dog treats. My pet begged for one-on-one time. Finally, I gave up and took him outside on the patio, where he was content to sit in silence by my side on a cozy glider.

As I succumbed to relaxing and enjoying the solitude, an "aha" moment just about whacked me over the head. I consistently denied myself a time out. Indeed, the advice I dole out to others should also apply to me.

Deepak Chopra writes about "The Law of Pure Potentiality" in his book *The Seven Spiritual Laws of Success*. He teaches we must take time each day to connect with our spirit. How many times have I read in The Bible to "be still and listen," yet here I was thwarting a wise practice. That day I stayed on the patio for a very long time. Zolton happily watched the whitetail bunnies chase each other while I allowed the surroundings' peacefulness to soak deep into my soul.

Unplugging from the noise of the world offers numerous benefits. By observing silence daily, your stress level lowers. Cultivating quiet time brings you a greater sense of personal awareness. Gaining a deeper understanding of who you are spills over into creating more robust relationships. The practice of quiet time can even improve your sleep patterns.

Now, like clockwork, my canine friend reminds me to observe quiet time. I know better than to talk myself out it and acknowledge I am a happier person for practicing silence. Moreover, my dog likes me better too.

# Grace on Ice

My Canadian-born husband is wild about hockey. I'm wild about that Canadian, but hockey, not so much. In our home, numerous conversations revolve around the game, well mostly, he talks, and I listen politely, faking interest.

One day John related a hockey story that caught my attention. The Anaheim Ducks overpowered the Vancouver Canucks. At the point when the scoreboard revealed a 7 – 1 Ducks lead, the players were called off the ice by the team's manager and given strict instructions on how to deal with any further scoring. No celebratory gestures were to be displayed. A small smile was permitted, but only when the scoring player reached the bench. My husband explained that during the last three minutes of the game, when the score was 9-1, the Ducks made no attempt at further goals and just passed the puck around to run down the clock.

I've heard stories of good sportsmanship, but in my book, this game was exemplary. Whether on the ice or skating through everyday life, it is our responsibility to display appropriate behaviors. We live in a competitive society and continuously teach our children to strive and reach the top. There is another lesson to role model for our kids involving winning. Victory is sweet and should be savored, but not at the humiliation of another individual or group. By holding back on the hugs and high-fives, the Ducks demonstrated a powerful life lesson. Having the grace to refrain from adding shame to a frustrating loss, and gently letting the other team exit to lick their wounds without further embarrassment was an inspirational act of kindness and a strategy earning respect.

Good sportsmanship is also essential in the business arena. Zappos is a company known for treating both employees and customers with respect. This organization takes the lead in treating competitors with grace and dignity. Staff members at Zappos are trained to help a customer find a product at a competitor's store if need be. That's pretty impressive, right?

Take a moment and think about how you treat your competition. Are you keeping your actions and dialogue regarding your rivals honest and above board, or are you involved in a cutthroat, winner-take-all battle? Do you go the extra mile and offer advice to others trying to enter your field? Would you refer a client to a competitor if you could not fulfill their need? Challenge yourself to display a little more grace and good sportsmanship in your life. Your actions will get noticed, and your respect rating will rise.

# Inspiration

In Summary:

- Be the missing link
- Create a life list
- Capture creative thoughts
- Push the boundaries
- Extend grace
- Observe silence daily
- Engage in self-coaching
- Cross some lines
- Bond with positive people

# Communication Connection is Key

"The difference between the right word
and the almost right word is the difference
between lightning and a lightning bug."

— Mark Twain

# To Speak, Or Be Silent

THE OTHER DAY MY FRIENDS, Becky and LaRita, asked me to weigh-in on a discussion involving when to hold your tongue and when to speak your truth. Great question. We've all been there. You're having a conversation with someone, and they say something that offends you. Do you call them out on it, or let it go?

I chimed in by using a prayer I recite every morning as my guide, "Help me act firmly and wisely without embittering or embarrassing others." There is much to unpack in these words, so let's break it down.

Most importantly, act wisely. Refrain from letting your tongue make the decision. If the remark has a sting to it, it may not have been the speaker's intent. Make the adage "give the other party the benefit of the doubt" your first consideration.

Next, ask yourself if the subject of the discussion is worth a deeper dive. Stated differently, should you change the subject, or continue on the same path? If it's a trivial matter, do yourself a favor and let it go. Perhaps the speaker was having a rotten day and not thinking clearly about how his or her words might be perceived. Be kind in your evaluation of the circumstance.

Now let's examine the flip side. Perhaps the speaker, who could be a friend or a co-worker, habitually tosses out ill-conceived or inaccurate thoughts with no inkling of the consequences. You need not be a doormat. By "acting firmly," you can put an end to the dialog of an inconsiderate individual. But before you take on the task, put some serious thought into time, place, and words.

In a group discussion, you risk embarrassing the guilty party in front of others, not an acceptable option. Plan a one-on-one. Don't speak in vague generalities, thoughtfully discuss a specific situation and let the individual know how the words made you feel.

Lastly, the person will either get it or not. Best-case scenario, you receive an apology. Be forewarned; not everyone takes constructive criticism well. You might receive a defensive reply. Tread softly here. You've said your piece now say no more and avoid "embittering" the person. Have an exit strategy prepared and close the conversation with a hug or a handshake if possible. If not, know you've done your best.

A final word, whether you hold your tongue or speak your truth, I recommend ending the conflict with an act of forgiveness on your part. After that, you can move on to the sunnier side of life.

# Want More Ice Cream? Just Ask!

AFTER READING ONE OF MY favorite motivational speakers' blogs, I decided to heed his advice and give it a try. Darren Hardy, success mentor, author, and keynote speaker convinced me of the adage, "If you don't ask you don't get." Sounds simple enough, I know, but you must understand I'm a rule follower. If the sign displays a price of $75.00, it never occurs to me there might be wiggle room.

Darren illustrated his point in a blog about an experience in an ice cream parlor. When he got down to the cone after eating a luscious scoop of vanilla, his taste buds screamed for more. He charmed the clerk into adding a "small gratuitous shaving to the top" to help extend his joy. Seriously I thought? I would never dream of making such a request. Apparently, this guy is super charming because the clerk replied it would be her pleasure. Wow!

I was ready to give this a go, so the very next night at a dinner meeting, I took the plunge. Dessert was chocolate mousse. As a rule, I do not eat dessert; however, I thought a cookie would be a fun treat. When a wait-staff member passed, using my sweetest and most pleasant manner, I asked if there was a cookie in the kitchen with my name on it. He replied that he would check, but never returned. I was not surprised nor discouraged, just rather pleased with myself for trying.

Next, I tackled my cell phone bill. Last month I was charged a $20 premium due to some kind of texting overage. I called the nice man at AT&T and told him I wanted my plan to include unlimited texting. He quoted me a rate of $25 more than my base rate. Okay, this wasn't working, so I mentioned regretfully that I must change carriers. At this point, he told me he could sell me a different plan retaining the benefits of my current program and including unlimited texting for $20 less than my base rate. Truly this made even less sense, but who was I to question the wisdom of the mega-giant who supplies me with minutes? Sold! Thanks to Mr. Hardy, I am now saving $20 every month and utilizing the text feature with no penalties.

Are you withholding your voice and accepting face value? Try speaking up this week for what you want. It doesn't always work, but I can tell you from recent practice it's a challenge worth pursuing. I'm getting good at this. Just wait until Santa sees my Christmas wish list!

# 'Tis the Season to Be Memorable

I SPENT THE FIRST HOUR of the cookie swap party painfully ignoring the vast array of plated sweets and listening to one friend after another. I'm good at listening and everything that goes along with it. I'm attentive, polite, always making good eye contact, and adept at showing a sincere interest in others. No doubt, that is why I chose career coaching as a profession.

Quite frankly, after about sixty minutes of absorbing everyone's news, woes, and updates, I began bordering on input overload. In a fortuitous turn of events, an unknown woman with a deep throaty laugh crossed my path. She was new to the area, and after explaining a bit about herself, she began peppering me with a few deep-rooted questions. Talk about showing an interest; this woman could hold court with Oprah! She had a fantastic knack for engaging me in a conversation that rapidly surpassed small talk. My new friend gracefully conversed without dominating the dialog, allowing me to walk away from our meeting feeling refreshed and content. At the end of our discussion, we exchanged business cards, and I excused myself so she could continue meeting new people and assimilating into the group.

Holiday season parties or any casual gatherings provide multiple opportunities to socialize, reunite with old friends, and encounter new people. To be remembered at an event long after the attendees go home, you must understand the guest list of any social function is composed of extroverts and introverts. If you're incredibly extroverted, you may want to monitor the amount of airtime typically captured by your outgoing nature. Try asking more questions and doing more listening. Challenge yourself to make it easy for the other person to speak. Showing an interest in someone else has a boomerang effect; eventually, the conversation bounces back to you.

If you are a bit on the shy side and worried about attending a party where you know only the host, build your confidence by preparing in advance. Get in a party mood by playing your favorite music as you travel to your destination. Brush up on being a master conversationalist by making a list of icebreaker topics such as a recent movie you liked, a book you read, or exciting travel stories. Experts say arriving early also helps qualm your nerves.

Whether you are a party animal, a Toastmaster extraordinaire, or as bashful as that cute little dwarf in Snow White, plan to have fun. Share the airtime, ask insightful questions, and smile.

# Golden Communication

WORDS CARRY IMMENSE POWER. THAT'S why I favor writing over speaking. As my fingers fly over the keyboard, I can add, delete, edit, and re-edit selecting the ideal words to convey my exact meaning. But when it comes to opening my mouth, sometimes the wrong words tumble out. Once that happens, there is no way to retrieve them.

I'm not just referring to sentences spewed in a fit of anger. Certainly, hurtful words cause immense pain and tend to rebound, doubling the damage. If you're prone to quickly releasing a tongue lashing, I caution you against engaging in dialog until you've given the consequences some serious consideration.

Let's focus on words used in everyday life that make a negative impression on others. For example, I know a kind of a "woe is me" individual, whose favorite catch-phrase is, "You just don't understand." She asserts this mantra frequently signaling her friends could not possibly feel the depth of her emotion. Her words convey that listeners are either too stupid or not worldly enough to relate to her situation. If she analyzed the effect her dialogue produces, she might eliminate that phrase from her vocabulary.

Ever try to turn the tide by making a process change within a group? If you did, I'm betting you heard my pet peeve, "We cannot change because this is the way it's always been done." Upon hearing those words, I want to throw up my hands and storm away. Why? Because it signals avoidance to try doing something different and thus rejects the possibility of a beneficial change. A prime example of negative speak is, "I can't," or "It's impossible." Perhaps we all let those words slip off our tongue too easily.

Think about phrases containing negatives. Ever offer sincere thanks to someone and get a "no problem" in reply? I'm guessing at least ten times per day, right? Wouldn't you rather hear, "You are most welcome," or "It was my pleasure." I know I would.

Communication is a skill. If you want to master it, make it a point to inventory your vocabulary. Effective communication means omitting negative phrases you say more out of habit than purpose and clearly conveying a message that builds trust in relationships. Measure your words and speak them to represent a specific intent. Lastly, rather than rattle off empty sentences to fill a void, consider silence. Often it really is golden.

# And Now, a Word From Your Parents

EACH SEPTEMBER, AS I THINK about America's youth returning to school, I recall a letter my mother sent me during my first week in college. Putting pen to paper was a sage move on her part because, like most first-year college students, I listened to my parents' verbal counsel with only half an ear. I cannot recall the exact advice she doled out, but I do remember reading the letter, saving it, and then reading it repeatedly.

The first day of school brings up all kinds of emotions for parents. You are excited as your kids embark on a new journey, and if you are sincere, a little sad to see them go. Perhaps you and your child prepared in advance for the big day. I remember when my niece Aisalynn was starting kindergarten. All summer long, she and her little friend Anna practiced skipping naps. Why? Because there are no naps in kindergarten. Starting school means playing in the big leagues. Backpacks and new Hello Kitty lunchboxes stood ready for weeks before the big day arrived. These two youngsters could hardly wait for the school bell to ring.

Whether your offspring is in the starting blocks anxious to hit the ground running, or filled with trepidation about the transition, it is your job to send them off prepared. In addition to supplying them with pencil cases, calculators, and laptops, you also need to dispense some reliable parental guidance. If they are starting school for the first time, talk to them about making friends by smiling and introducing themselves to other children. Keep rein over your emotions. Don't let your kindergartener see a tear inching down your face as you part at the classroom door. It will only sadden and confuse them.

Adolescent children may need an extra dose of emotional support. Work with them by instituting a time management program to prevent oversleeping that leads to a stressful start. Encourage your pre-teen and teenage children to set goals for the school year. Create schedules for homework, outside activities, and some "me" time for your child.

If you are dropping your son or daughter off at the dorm, forget the lectures. He or she probably won't absorb it anyway. Try doing it the old fashioned way. Write a heartfelt letter. Stick to just a few pieces of sage advice, enclose it in a fun greeting card (money helps too), and send it snail mail. With any luck, your child might not only read it but also take it to heart and incorporate your parental wisdom into college life.

# Make Your Vision
# a Reality

WHEN I FIRST HEARD ABOUT vision boards, my brain's right and left side began a battle. If you are unfamiliar with the concept of a vision board, some say creating one helps manifest things you want in your life. (I get it if you are rolling your eyes right now, thinking what kind of woo-woo stuff is this?) My right lobe knew I was attracted to magazines with glossy, colorful pictures. Since childhood, I loved cutting, pasting, and day-dreaming, so why not create a vision board? The left side of my brain countered that posting pictures on cardboard with hopes of making dreams come true was utterly illogical. I let the point, counterpoint go on for a while, and finally decided it made sense to take a middle-of-the-road approach and give it a try.

I created a vision board to help me expand my thought process. Every twelve-month period is too beautiful a gift to waste. Designing a board with impressive glossy images aided in forming my plan for the future. Centering my board on a theme helped me whittle down my broad vision to a few main objectives. My vision board for last year was entitled, "The Year of Completion." Why? Because I started several projects that did not reach the finish line until I zeroed in on them daily. Having my vision board front and center kept me committed.

This year I expanded the process. My favorite coach, Jen Altieri, invited me to her Vision Board Workshop. Jen, the founder of Hope Inrheart Life Coaching, began the class by stating, "Many benefits of a vision board come from the process in which it was created. Believe it or not, there is more to it than gluing pictures to a board." Jen drilled down on the process by explaining, "It is about setting intentions for whom you will become and what you will do as much as it is about what you will have. Only after you have this clarity is it time to cut and paste. Until we know what it is we want, we can't receive it."

She invited us to spend some quiet time on the grounds of her lovely south Florida home to work on a soul-searching exercise created especially for this workshop. (Lounging in an Adirondack chair as the sun warmed my back, I realized the value of this workshop and vowed to attend every year.) When we were ready, we filed back in the meeting room to create our visual plan for the next 12 months. Afterward, we proudly held up our boards and posed for a photo op.

Jen closed the session by reminding us that, "Vision boards give your mind permission to dream in alignment with your heart. What we put our attention on grows in our life. That's why focusing daily on vision boards helps move our pictures from dreams to reality."

Altieri is in good company. Jack Canfield, best-selling author, motivational speaker, and corporate trainer, professes that our brains will work tirelessly to achieve the statement we give our subconscious mind. Canfield believes, "When those statements are the affirmations and images of our goals, we are destined to achieve them!"

Whether you are trying to change careers, start a business, write a book, travel to Paris in springtime, or get in shape, it pays to repeat a kindergarten process. Take out the scissors and glue and create your vision. Then, boldly hang it as a visual reminder. If you can see it, you can do it!

# Listen Up!

RECENTLY MY FRIEND BARB AND I attended a brunch seminar. Later we met up with our spouses and related stories told by the fascinating keynote speaker. About halfway through Barb's rendition of the presentation, I realized we were both at the same meeting, and yet, she heard more of the story than I. No, there is nothing wrong with my hearing. I knew what happened. I lost focus.

I think I am an attentive listener, but that morning I was not mindfully engaged. Thoughts ping-ponged around in my head during the presenter's time on stage.

Shouldn't listening to a captivating speech be an easy singular task? Not so, according to Marty Nemko, a coach who holds a Ph.D. from the University of California, Berkley. Marty claims listening is tougher than people think. I believe Marty is right. Listening requires effort, sometimes a lot of it.

A friend of mine once stated, "We are in the listening business. All-day long, we listen to others." That's true, our lives and jobs depend on listening, so perhaps sometimes we get tired of all the words coming at us. Okay, but none of us can afford to get lazy about listening.

How can we improve this skill? For starters, we can either listen out of generosity or curiosity. The latter is the better choice, and Barb proved it. She had more takeaways from the program because she was tuned-in. So if we listen with a curious ear, we benefit because we learn.

As a reminder, listening takes discipline. When I chose to attend the brunch, I wanted to experience every part of the agenda. During the speech, I allowed my mind to drift. Perhaps I was tired, or lulled into a mild stupor by the meal; however, the point is, I permitted myself to cease listening. Don't let yourself off the hook, discipline your mind to stay present in the moment. When you find your thoughts straying from the subject at hand, put yourself back in. I promised myself next time I found my concentration slipping; I would take a deep breath and refocus.

My best advice on listening is credited to iconic radio host Larry King who said, "I remind myself every morning. Nothing I say this day will teach me anything. So if I'm going to learn, I must do it by listening."

# Communication

- Engage in negotiation
- Inventory your vocabulary
- Listen generously
- Create a vision board
- Share your wisdom
- Show interest in others
- Become a master conversationalist
- Chose your words wisely
- Speak up

# Attitude
# Check Your
# Temperament

"The greatest discovery of all time is that
a person can change his future
by merely changing his attitude."

— OPRAH WINFREY

# It's Your Picnic

ONE OF MY FAVORITE CLIENTS is a busy entrepreneur who does a significant amount of networking throughout the city. Her calendar fills up with mixers, meetings, and other events that keep her on the go practically seven days per week. Granted, she is an extremely high-energy, upbeat individual, but I know at times weariness sets in, and she would rather hunker down to watch a ballgame with her husband or binge Netflix a bit.

Curious as to how she maintains the momentum, I implored her to share the secret. It's all about attitude was her answer. By employing the mantra "bring your own weather to the picnic," a quote made famous by author Harlan Coben, my client always spends a moment preparing before entering the event.

We can all take a page from her book and share in the picnic philosophy. Think about a recent dreaded calendar commitment you experienced. Mentally rewind the event and take an honest look at your behavior. Did you drag yourself through the front door with a half-hearted smile plastered on your face? While in attendance, were you checking your watch every ten minutes, wondering when it would be acceptable to make a mad dash for the exit? Are you guilty of eye rolling while an agenda item ricocheted around the room in a debate?

That kind of action is akin to bringing ants to the picnic. Determined not to enjoy and actively participate in the event, you sabotaged any chance to add value or receive any in return. My guess is we have all done that from time to time.

Let's take the same dreaded event and create a new script. This time we will practice a little self-talk as a preventative measure to ensure a positive experience. Why is the meeting on your calendar? I am assuming you have a valid reason for agreeing to participate. Perhaps the problem arose because the meeting fell at the end of a day that found you suffering severe exhaustion induced by jumping through hoops to meet a rush project deadline.

We cannot always control the calendar, but we can stop and take a breath. Acknowledge that you must honor your meeting commitment. Observe silence for a full five minutes. Just let your mind float to a happier place. Next, begin to conjure up three valid reason to make the most of the experience. It might be the opportunity to learn something new, meet an interesting person, and chime in on an important decision. Employ this strategy, and you are ready to attend the picnic equipped with fair skies and no ants.

# Hot Doggin It

FROM THE COMFORT OF MY living room, I watched the LA Angels play the Minnesota Twins. To say it was wicked hot in Target Field that day was no exaggeration. Spectators fanned themselves, sucked on snow cones and downed ice-cold beer and lemonade to ward off the oppressive heat.

During the game, the camera zoomed in on a hot dog vendor. I watched in amazement as he patiently created curly mustard art over the tubed meat. Okay, sounds like a small thing, I know, but if I were standing in the blazing sun while schlepping around a large metal case loaded with hot dogs, buns, mustard, and relish, I'm pretty sure I would have quickly smeared the yellow condiment and moved on to my next customer. But, not this guy. With flair, flourish, and the right attitude, he presented the fan with the perfect hot dog and a great customer experience.

Thinking about the hot dog guy reminded me of my first job in human resources. My manager was wonderful, but the position was rather boring. Carving out a successful career in HR was the goal, but the starting point offered no challenge. One day I stumbled across these two sentences, "The way you do one thing is how you do everything. Be aware." Reading those lines rocked my small corporate world. You see, if the job was mind-numbing, it was my own doing.

To make the work exciting and my job valuable, I needed to change my perspective and create a challenge. Conducting a serious meeting with myself in the drab green cubicle, where I spent most of the working day, I decided to make some changes. I began by hanging motivational posters to keep me inspired. Then I set a schedule to complete my workload in five hours and spend the rest of my day assisting others, creating projects that added value to the department, and if time remained working on my personal development. By the end of the week, the tide had turned. Now I was the first person in the office and often the last one out the door at night. I was transitioning an entry-level job into a position with substance and challenge that launched my career.

The bottom line, when you receive a task, embrace it! Whether it's using mustard as a creative art form to delight the customer or entering employee information into a database, give it your all, and put your unique spin on it. Being aware of "how you do one thing," will help you make a difference.

# Is That Your Real Smile?

WHEN I FIRST HEARD THE expression, "fake it 'til you make it," I shuddered. Acting falsely seemed so disingenuous. But, sometime after, I experienced a light-bulb moment prompting me to find some value in revisiting the act of presenting a false front.

Perhaps it was the Dale Carnegie course I took decades ago. Before delivering a two-minute speech, a speaker was to stand at the back of the room, and upon being introduced, run up the aisle clapping and acting enthusiastic. Let me repeat those keywords: acting enthusiastic. Trust me, when I stood at the back of the room preparing to take the spotlight, I felt anything but enthusiastic. Terrified, mortified and horrified maybe, but far from excited about public speaking. After the 12-week course came to a close, I realized the Carnegie people had it right. Forcing yourself to smile, clap, and jog your way to the front of the room helped minimize the jitters. Drawing yourself up, pulling your shoulders back, and remembering to take a few deep breaths aids in conjuring up a smattering of self-confidence.

My older and wiser self still gives credence to the "fake it 'til you make it" maxim, but I would temper that piece of wisdom by advising you can take the acting element only so far.

Did you know many people can spot a fake smile? According to Psychology Today, a fake smile is evidenced by a contraction of the zygomatic major muscle. A genuine grin, dubbed a "Duchenne" smile, named after the French doctor Guillaume Duchenne, a student of the physiology of facial expressions, involves both voluntary and involuntary contractions from the zygomatic major and the orbicularis oculi. Okay, enough geeky lingo, but think about that next time you plaster on your phony smirk when encountering your boastful bore of a brother-in-law, or any personality type you prefer to avoid.

What should you do when you're not feeling the love? Examine your motivation. If you have to spend an afternoon with your bigheaded brother-in-law to appease your wife, own it. Chase away the negative emotions by acknowledging you are doing something thoughtful for your spouse.

One last thought regarding zygomatic major and orbicularis oculi: These terms are challenging to pronounce and harder to remember. When a situation arises, making happiness a stretch, prepare yourself by focusing on a pleasant thought like your next vacation, a great evening, or a kiss from a loved one and smile, smile, smile. After doing so, your future smiles might not be fake at all.

# Controlling Your Emotional Reset

LISA ARRIVED AT OUR COFFEE date with a bright smile, but I sensed beneath the surface, something was bothering her. After we placed our order, I urged her to fess up. She sighed and admitted people had been pushing her buttons all week. When I inquired about the culprits, she gave me a list beginning with her boss, her sister, and of course, the woman at the mall. I could not help but laugh. We have a standing joke about the vendor at the mall that hawks anti-aging products. She has a habit of zeroing in on your weakest feature as you pass by, making you cringe when she loudly exclaims her magic elixir fixes your neck or whatever body part is succumbing to gravity.

Buttons require little explanation. We all have sensitive areas that make us emotionally volatile. One forceful push throws us off balance. Instantly we begin feeling negative, insecure, or just plain angry.

Lisa told me the other day she proudly turned in a complex work project ahead of schedule hoping for an atta-girl, as a small consideration that her hard work was valued. Instead of a pat on the back, she received her manager's intelligible grunt and another assignment. She returned to her desk, fuming over the lack of appreciation.

I stepped in to help my friend sort this out. Never before had Lisa cast her boss in a negative light. I inquired if her timing was off, suggesting perhaps she entered his office at an inopportune moment. After some consideration, Lisa revealed that her leader had just returned from a three-hour meeting with the corporate CFO. I suggested she chalk this one up to what was going on in his world and not take it personally.

Regarding her sister, siblings are notorious for button-pushing because they know precisely where our soft spots lie. Lisa and I discussed her sister's offhanded remarks. We agreed she would set boundaries letting her sibling know precisely what is off-limits. By telling her sister what she does is offensive, Lisa can stop this barb-flinging habit.

As far as the woman at the mall goes, there is a solution. Lisa can try the product (who knows, it might work) or not cross directly in front of the store.

Who's pushing your buttons? Do some soul searching today and decide on the best way to deal with your reactions. Take control, sort it out then push your reset button before those negative emotions begin festering.

# Pretend You're
# From New Jersey

DURING THE PAST FEW WEEKS, I've heard several people brag about character traits they attribute to "being from New Jersey." After putting some thought into it, I wondered if upbringing in a particular geographic location brings with it an acquired persona.

Thinking of strong personalities that hail from The Garden State, I reviewed the styles of John Travolta, Joe Pesci, former governor Chris Christie, and Queen Latifah. Yep, definitely a pattern there. Entrepreneur Marie Forleo, named by Oprah as "the thought leader for the next generation," who recently proclaimed the "New Jersey brag," caught my attention. She is self-described as: "part business strategist, part marketing maven and part spiritual ass-kicker with a side of hip-hop swagger." Upon learning Marie created a multi-million dollar socially conscious empire from scratch, I decided to drill down. What does being born and bred in New Jersey offer other than favorite sons like Bruce Springsteen, Jon Bon Jovi, Frank Sinatra, and my favorite baseball legend LA Angel, Mike Trout?

Diving headfirst into my research, I discovered people from Jersey (that's how they like to refer to it Jersey, not Joisey, that offends them) know the location of every clip shown in the Sopranos opening credits and brag about producing the best pizza. Never do our New Jersey friends pump their gas because it's illegal in their state. They have lots of Jersey pride, but more importantly, they have attitude. (I even discovered a song on YouTube called Jersey Attitude). Many Jerseyan's claim to be intense, clearly driven, focused, and not afraid of much. That last trait meshed with a study done by the Journal of Personality and Social Psychology, finding our Jersey friends uninhibited.

In contrast, my birth state is Michigan. Of course, we have bragging rights too. Just watch a "Pure Michigan" travel ad, and you will see the majesty of the Great Lake state. Ask me to name all five of the Great Lakes and point to their locations around my left and right hand, and I'll give you a tour. But in my experience, the New Jersey chutzpah is somewhat foreign to the Michigan culture. (Although I think Governor Gretchen Whitmer, a born and bred Michigander, has a real Jersey vibe going.)

I must admit there are days I wish I possessed the blatant daring of our New Jersey counterparts. Attitude is defined as "a way of thinking or feeling about something or someone reflected in a person's behavior." Surely it wouldn't hurt to add a little attitude to my current persona. So here goes, this week, I'm kicking my mild Michigander roots to the curb, turning a blind eye to what others think, stepping up to speak my truth, vowing to take a leap of faith with no regrets and adding a definite swagger.

# Is the Customer Always Right?

You've experienced it, and so have I. Sooner or later, we all must deal with those annoying clients who make us nuts. You know the type. She's the one who makes you want to take cover when you see her name pop up on your cell phone or incoming email list. They come in all varieties. Some take advantage of the relationship by constantly wanting more than stipulated in a contract or agreement. Graciously you give in, and after a cursory thank you, they ask for more.

Others do not practice honesty, have no sense of integrity, and will outright lie to you. Their payments are always late, claiming they ran out of checks or firing off one of the 99 other excuses that readily slip off their tongue. The question is, how we keep from tearing our hair out when difficult personalities cross our path?

I don't know much about Zen, other than it is a way of being; however, I recently stumbled across a helpful Zen principle called the "beginners mind." The premise, eliminate prejudging the individual's situation. Stated differently, stop thinking the "shoulds," like they "should" understand the contract. Those "shoulds" bouncing around in our heads make us defensive and unproductive. Remedy this by "tapping into the beginner's mind" and start again. Take a breath and summon up your highest professional self. Explain the contract, or the payment terms in detail until the client acknowledges understanding.

Here's something to put on the "don't" side of the ledger. Utilize the Dale Carnegie philosophy, "Why prove to a man he is wrong? Is that going to make him like you? Why not let him save face?" Deal with this disgruntled individual by acknowledging it may be your fault for not explaining the contract clearly. Sure, you know he's wrong, but rubbing it in his face accomplishes nothing.

What about the impossible client who consistently disregards deadlines putting you behind? You know their modus operandi, so change your timeline. Overestimating the time it will take to complete a job will help keep you on track.

Lastly, it helps to recognize conflict is part of doing business. There is some truth in the adage, "the customer is always right." The flip side is, you can always fire the client. It is okay to do so, but it is a bit tricky. Do it gracefully without burning your bridges.

Bottom line, if you intend to keep working with that impossible client, lean in, use the strategies I outlined, and call on your better angels to help you suck it up and get the job done.

# It's all in the Approach

DON'T YOU LOVE IT WHEN you have all the right moves? Yep, so do I, but let's get serious for a moment. Having the perfect answer is a start, but it's the right approach that lands us a win. For example, do you think your 13-year-old son is listening as you stomp around and use your outdoor voice while chastising him for not cleaning his room? Heck no. He's tuning you out and sending a message back loud and clear as he scowls and rolls his eyes. You see, he can't hear you, when you are too loud.

But I'm not writing to give parenting advice. Our subject involves behavior modification, yours and mine. Someone once said, "Not every single way of saying the right thing is right." But if we could get the approach right every single time, we'd get what we need.

Getting your teen to clean his room, or convincing anyone to do what you want, may not be easy. It involves the art of gentle persuasion. Cracking the code on how to get your way and create a winning situation calls for some strategic techniques and lots of practice.

We can all begin by controlling the level of our emotions. When using a calm approach, we stand a much better chance of getting attention, which proceeds getting agreement. The advice your mom probably said repeatedly, "You can catch more flies with honey than with vinegar," is golden. Reaching out with a pleasant approach frames your influence.

If you told your son he acts like he lives in a pigsty, you're probably doing it wrong. (Thus the persistent eye rolls). We all need to feel good about who we are. Change up your approach: no shaming or embarrassing others.

To master the win, practice editing your speech. Do a dry run in your head before opening your mouth. How does it sound? Would you agree to keep a neat environment, or accept a work assignment if someone used that rhetoric? Remember also to consider body language. Your sugar-sweet words won't be respected if you are frowning poised with your hands on your hips. Be authentic by slapping a smile on your face and in your voice.

One last thought. The word please never goes out of style. Two words that take the sting out of an unwelcome task are "please and thank-you." Remember, you're in control. You get to choose the right approach. Do so with the end result in mind.

# Attitude

In Summary:

- Control your emotions
- Edit your speech
- Consider timing
- Set boundaries
- Create a challenge
- Examine your motivation
- Call on your better angels
- Observe silence and regroup
- Swagger a bit

# Kindness
# Grace and Goodness

"This best part of life is not just surviving but
thriving with passion and compassion and humor
and style and generosity and kindness."

— MAYA ANGELOU

# My Big Five

I DON'T ALWAYS GET IT right. That was pretty obvious last week when I opened a thank you email. Although I was happy to be the recipient of some gratitude, color me ashamed of myself. You see I extended a stranger a professional courtesy, no charge, no strings attached, just to be helpful and practice kindness. Later I grumbled in my head for at least 48 hours about the silence. Where was a show of appreciation?

After this experience, I recognized two facts. My act of kindness wasn't "no strings attached." I have a habit of expecting immediate gratitude in response when I should give for the sake of giving. A genuine and sincere giver expects nothing in return. Not only did I want a "thanks a lot," I wanted it in my defined timeframe. When I didn't get it, I let my thoughts yammer on about allowing others to take advantage of me.

My attitude changed when I read this line from a prayer: "Blessed are those who give without expecting anything in return." Okay, got the message. I needed to change my expectations. When I pondered this quote from Timber Hawkeye, it put me to shame: "Give without expecting anything in return. That is unconditional kindness...everything else is ego." Oh, I am so busted. Wanting something in return was a way to feed my big fat ego.

I decided to teach myself a lesson by putting some thought into overcoming my desire for give and take. By doing my homework, I came up with several life lessons to put into action.

If you've ever been to a second grader's softball game, you may have noticed no one keeps score. Using that philosophy to begin a list of corrective action items, I wrote, "Throw away the scoreboard." Coupling my new rule with a familiar phrase, I also jotted down, "pay it forward." As the beneficiary of kind acts, I underlined that one twice.

Often my expectations run high. Had I given freely, with no agenda, the thank you email would have been a sweet surprise. Number three on my list was "set no expectations." Then another thought occurred to me. There is no such thing as too much kindness. Why did I offer up a deed and then feel someone was taking advantage of my good nature? Quickly I penned my number four, "Give, give and give some more."

Five seems like a good number, so the last item refers to being my best self, who I want to be daily. Any success I've experienced in my career was because I took my job seriously. Got it! My fifth and final rule is, "It is my job to be kind."

The good news is, I've been getting it right lately and realize there is an inherent payback. The act of giving provides me with an enhanced sense of peace, love, and joy. Thankfully, that is more than enough.

# The Fine Art of Praise

MY FRIEND MELISSA IS ONE of the most generous people I know. She blessed my life and those of many others in a notable manner. Melissa never misses an opportunity to lavish sincere praise when she finds it fitting. Not only does she express her kindness to others by issuing compliments, but Melissa does so in a meaningful way.

The other day I was the recipient of one of Melissa's bighearted gifts. She attended a presentation I gave at a business meeting. Not only did she absorb and remember the message I delivered, the next morning, when I visited my Facebook page, Melissa also tagged me in a post. Other friends might have sent me a quick private message telling me they enjoyed my presentation. Not Melissa. She wrote a lengthy paragraph of "shout out" praise to be viewed by friends and clients on social media. Her act of kindness was generous and an example of how Melissa goes out of her way to lift up people, making them feel special.

Generosity is the virtue of giving freely and abundantly. Sometimes we offer time, in other instances, money or material goods. People like Melissa find innovative ways to make the world a brighter place.

Khalil Gibran professed, "Generosity is giving more than you can and taking less than your need." Wise words to live by, and conversely, we can all identify acquaintances, perhaps even family members, who either refrain or rarely think to offer up an "atta boy."

In my coaching practice, I often encounter individuals who talk about never receiving a compliment from a parent, sibling, or even their boss. Denying a deserving person a word of praise is the opposite of being generous. Withholding admiration consistently can also be a form of emotional punishment.

Not everyone is as highly skilled as Melissa in the art of a compliment. If you are holding back praising others because it feels awkward or fear doing it wrong, just practice. Start small. Try telling your boss you like her dress (if you do). Next, try focusing on characteristics and skills. Perhaps your coworker wrote an excellent procedure shortcutting a task and making your work-life easier. Applaud that action, verbally, in writing or at a staff meeting in front of the boss.

There is only one rule when passing out compliments. Be sincere. Coupling sincerity with generosity will make your tribute memorable.

# One of the Ten Best Gifts

IT WAS UNEXPECTED BUT CAME at a time when I needed it most. The entire week was fraught with sadness and deep sorrow for my family due to my brother's death. As I trudged to the mailbox expecting nothing but bills and catalogs plastered with holiday gift ideas, I found a small pink envelope. While observing the soft hue and scanning lovely cursive penmanship dictating my address, I felt an inner warmth. Somewhere during a week weighted down with gloomy gray clouds, a sliver of light was on the horizon.

Returning to my office, I slit the envelope and read the one-page note. It was a thank you letter of sorts from a reader of my newspaper column. She acknowledged something I do weekly, never knowing who might benefit, but hoping people do. This letter is going down in my book as one of "The Ten Bests Gifts I Ever Received."

Want to give a special gift to touch the heart of a friend or loved one, and perhaps make their top ten list? Read on; I'll walk you through it. Pick up a pen or station yourself behind your keyboard. Close your eyes and do a deep dive into how your chosen one adds value to your life. Express sincere gratitude for something specific. Think beyond material gifts and write a paragraph on how their actions make your world a better place. Don't worry about writing style, find your voice, and communicate your feelings.

After performing this written exercise, I would not be surprised if you decided to do another, and then another. While researching gratitude letters, I stumbled upon an article about a fellow named John Kralik. In 2008, he made a New Year's resolution to write one thank you note each day. He created notes to family, friends, co-workers, and even the barista at Starbucks.

Taking it one step further, Kralik turned his notes into a book, *365 Thank Yous: The Year a Simple Act of Daily Gratitude Changed My Life*. John succinctly provides advice on writing a thank you to this, "Focus on one true meaningful sentence about the person." Kralik also recommends you do it the old school way. You know, with pen and paper.

My favorite word of advice from the author is keeping the thank you so short and simple that it could fit on a 3" x 5" notecard. Why? So there is no room in your gift for anything but gratitude.

Ready to give it a go? I'm trusting your note will deliver more joy than you can imagine.

# A Different Kind of Gift

A NUMBER OF MY FRIENDS love online tests. You know what I'm talking about, right? For example, the Color Personality Test, How Old Do You Really Act Test and the What Should Your Parents Have Named You Test. (I got Emma by the way).

Well, I have a test for you. It's about gift-giving. Coincidentally, this is my birthday month, and I can tell you precisely what will happen. My friend Nancy will give me some wonderfully practical item (last year it was organizers for my luggage) that I will keep forever. Janie will send me something lovely, but it will probably arrive in November. She has a loving, generous nature, but tends to run behind a bit. From my husband, it will be something he knows I want even though I never expressed it. He is perceptive that way.

My pal Samantha loves sweets. Whenever I go to her home, she greets me with a cocktail loaded with sugary fruity stuff. (The thing is, I am a savory.) Consequently, my gift from Samantha will probably be some luscious chocolate-fudgy something or other. Yes, she doesn't realize my preference, but she gifts me something she perceives as absolutely over-the-top, and I love her for it!

Birthdays are fun, and presents are great, but let's get serious for a moment and talk about a different kind of gift. Rate yourself on the non-material gifts you offer the world. Are you generous with your compliments? Do you lavish praise on others, especially those who desire your approval. Are you taking the time to offer encouragement and a helping hand? Do you mentor and act as a role model for others? Do you give of your time and stay present in the moment when interacting with loved ones? Is gratitude high on your priority list?

If you passed this quiz with flying colors, I applaud you, but if you came in a little lean, no worries. We are all a work in progress. I'm making kindness a priority this year. I posted a sign on my Vision Board that says, "Kick up Your Kindness Level." One of the ways I am doing so is by using the website, More Love Letters.

The founder, Hannah Brencher, a Ted Speaker and blogger was my inspiration. Feeling lonely and depressed when she moved to New York City, this real-life hero did something about it. Hannah started writing and leaving love notes all over the city. She tucked them away in library books, coffee shops, and even bathroom stalls. You can read more about this kindness movement in her book, *If You Find This Letter: My Journey to Find Purpose Through Hundreds of Letters to Strangers.*

Each month I go to Hannah's website, www.moreloveletters.com, and write a love letter of sorts to someone who could use a dose of encouragement. If that act of kindness appeals to you, head over to her website now.

So this week, make it a point to shine your light on others. Caring acts bless both the giver and receiver. And thanks for being a loving change agent!

# Timely Kudos

ON A MISSION TO PURGE unwanted files, I filtered through the masses of paper in my office and unearthed an old "Warm and Fuzzy" file. The red folder contained cards and letters from family, friends, and employees. As I sifted through the contents, a small thank you card with a bear dancing in the sunshine caught my eye. Inside the author penned, "Thanks for noticing my hard work. Glad you head up our team." I smiled at the memory. Danielle, a member of my staff at the time, was indeed a dedicated employee.

Years ago, during my tenure as a new manager, I was influenced by multiple management gurus. In a book by Ken Blanchard and Spencer Johnson, *The One Minute Manager*, I first learned the value of "catching people doing something right." I often caught Danielle doing something right, which inspired her nod to me as her manager.

Although this management concept comes from a book published in the '80s, I believe wisdom is timeless. In a recent online article, Blanchard advises, "The best way to start this habit is to take an hour out of your week to walk around observing activity in your organization."

I agree with Ken. It's that easy, and it is a necessary kindness. Survey the workplace, and you will find employees adding value and driving business. The next logical step is acknowledgment. A word of warning here, a mumbled good job, or a robotic pat on the back won't cut it. There is an art to offering up effective praise. It must be sincere, meaningful, timely, and specific.

Whether you are trying to motivate employees and build a winning culture, or get your seven-year-old son to toss his dirty socks in the laundry hamper, place daily focus on catching "the right" actions. If your daughter cleans up her room, or your son takes out the garbage without your prodding and prompting, a gracious "thank you for being so considerate" and a lively high five will elicit pride and encourage continued positive behavior.

Think about making the concept universal. Catch people doing something right wherever you go. Enjoyed the impeccable dining service at your last girl's night out? Go one step beyond a generous tip and leave a complimentary review on Yelp mentioning the server's first name. My friend Irma asks to speak with the restaurant management and compliments him or her on a great hire. A final thought: Your words in a card or heartfelt email will go a long way and may even make it into someone's "Warm and Fuzzy" file.

# Aesop and The Mitzvah

OF COURSE, I KNOW WHAT a Bar Mitzvah is, but this week when a friend of mine told me a story of kindness and compassion, I learned another meaning of a "mitzvah." Kippy, who lived in Israel for years before returning to the United States, spoke about a particular Friday when her city was preparing for a festive Shabbat dinner. Inspired by mitzvah (which means commandment), the word also takes on the meaning of a charitable or beneficial act; she began thinking about the volunteer army and the uninteresting rations they would have for dinner.

If you met her, it would not take long before you realized she is a doer and a giver who is gifted with exceptional organizational skills. Armed with the knowledge that her community would soon be busy preparing the evening meal, she engaged each household in an impromptu project, and asked each family to make an extra meal for the nearby troops. She added a unique twist instructing each household chef to include his or her phone number in the food gift.

My friend understood it was a common practice to give anonymously, but something told her this act of kindness could evolve into more than a Friday night dinner. And she was right. Phones began ringing inside this small, gated community. Soldiers surprised and delighted with the homemade feasts reached out to share a greeting and thank their donors. What started as a standard Friday evening turned into a circle of goodwill thanks to Kippy.

I pondered her story thinking, like one of the infamous Aesop's Fables, the event includes a powerful moral. Although an anonymous kind deed is noble, sometimes we should be up close and personal with the recipient of our actions. Rabbi Lawrence Kushner, author, and Emanu-El Scholar quipped, "I think the poor man wants to know who's giving the gift, and the rich man wants to see the smile on the poor man's face.

Studies suggest that givers derive more from the act of giving than from the benefits their gifts generate for others. So why not borrow a page from Kippy's book. Think about reaching out in a personal manner to help a friend, a stranger, or a soldier. As Aesop taught in "The Lion and the Mouse," "No act of kindness, no matter how small, is ever wasted."

# Kindness

In Summary:

- No agendas
- Pay it forward
- No expectation
- Be generous with praise
- Be sincere
- Communicate your feelings
- Shine your light
- Acknowledge positive behavior
- Help others

# Fear
# Dealing With Doubt

"Never let the fear of striking out get in your way."

— BABE RUTH

# Eraser Magic

As I wished my eleven-year-old niece, Aisalynn, a happy birthday, my favorite pre-teen responded by telling me she really needed the eraser. Go figure. I sent a gift certificate to her favorite store, a book (my continuous agenda is to encourage reading) along with some silly, sparkly fake nails and a huge pink eraser shaped like a birthday cake. Who would have guessed the eraser was the biggest hit?

Later that day, it occurred to me an eraser is a "must-have" tool for a 5th grader. Those soft pink beveled erasers came in handy when you messed up on a math problem, misspelled a word, or had to remove the boy's name you had a crush on before your dad noticed it artfully displayed across your spelling notebook. I smiled wondering if an Aidan, a Caleb, or a Connor was Aisalynn's crush of the week.

Whether it's a blunder on a math test or bombing a job interview, mistakes happen. While you cannot erase away the actual evidence of a misstep, you can own it and profit from the experience. In my book, mistakes are as natural as breathing. My favorite quote on the subject is attributed to advertising executive Leo Burnett: "To swear off making mistakes is very easy. All you have to do is swear off having ideas."

Indeed mistakes range in severity. Some errors are mere speed bumps that bog you down on the road to victory. Others, like business bankruptcy, create noticeable failure, but whatever the blunder, recovery is possible. Need proof? Walt Disney declared bankruptcy in 1923 when he couldn't cover his studio's overhead. Five years later, he created a character named Mickey Mouse, and I don't need to tell you the rest of the story.

The key to a successful "do-over" is passion. Want an example? Well, look no further than your condiment shelf. When H.J. Heinz was 25, he founded a company that made horseradish, the firm tanked in 1875.

Not one to quit, Henry John reorganized and launched a new ketchup producing venture. Fun fact: As of this writing, Heinz now sells 640 million bottles of its iconic ketchup every year.

You can find the magic in making mistakes by considering the flip side. Analyze a current failure and list the lessons learned. Put a positive spin on the terminology. Rather than error, blunder, gaffe, or snafu, think of a problem as Henry J. Kaiser describes it, "An opportunity in work clothes."

If someone buys me an eraser for my birthday, I think I'll leave it on my desk as a reminder that failure is a gift called experience.

# Flight of Passion

THE ENTHUSIASTIC UBER DRIVER ENTERTAINED me by explaining his passion for soccer while shuttling me to the airport. Throughout the twenty-minute ride, I learned a good deal about the sport most countries, except the USA, refer to as football. Martin, my driver, who originally hails from Kenya, offered up at least seventeen reasons why soccer is the world's most popular sport. When I inquired how often he plays the game, he looked at me in his rearview mirror sheepishly. Meeting my puzzled expression, young Martin wistfully replied maybe someday, he'd get on the field again to boot the ball into the net.

While my plane departed from the gate, I pondered the reasons people fail to pursue their passions. Every 24 hours, we get an opportunity to push ourselves beyond the norm. Moving forward toward goals brings joy and immense personal satisfaction. So what stops us? Sure, we can feed ourselves the line that we are beyond busy, but we know that is just a lame excuse. I get that Martin was busy hustling up business, but I hoped that soon he could block out a few hours to get on the field.

Growing up, whenever I complained I was too busy to tackle a job, my mother stopped me in my tracks by reminding me that I could make the time to do it if I wanted something badly enough. Yes, dismissing my excuses with a little tough love worked wonders.

As a career coach, I find the fear of failure is often a stumbling block preventing individuals from pursuing their heart's desire. Sometimes looking at the big picture of a total career makeover is scary. My advice to anyone faced with a challenge appearing insurmountable is: Think small. That's right, small as in baby steps. Whether it's a career change, a move across the country, or tackling a remodel on your home, the magic begins when you break it down into actionable steps.

Another common lament involves confusion over where to begin. Professional tennis player Arthur Ashe put it best when he said, "Start where you are. Use what you have. Do what you can." Getting started need not be complicated. Take some time to brainstorm a path then commit it to writing. You can always make course corrections along the way. Just begin.

As I said good-bye to Martin at the airport, I offered up two tips. The first, a monetary thanks for his safe driving and soccer tutorial. My second tip, which I also offer anyone reading this is, stop stalling and take one of your "maybe someday dreams" and turn it into a reality. Start today in baby steps. I know you can do it!

# Change Your
# Definition of Failure

REMEMBER A TIME WHEN YOU missed the mark? You set a goal and, for one reason or another, failed to accomplish your dream. When faced with disappointment, our natural tendency is to experience the pain and eventually move on. Often we begin to see it as Shakespeare said, "What's done is done." Over the years, I learned a positive strategy: pause, reflect and refresh.

By pausing to rewind the experience and process the outcome, we discover the hidden benefits of failure.

In 2008, J.K. Rowling gave a commencement speech at Harvard entitled "The Fringe Benefits of Failure and the Importance of Imagination." Rowling contends she failed on an "epic scale" prior to becoming one of the most well known female authors based on her Harry Potter fantasy books. The series won multiple awards and sold over 500 million copies. During her Harvard speech, Rowling professed, "It is impossible to live without failing at something."

The author was intimately friendly with failure. Rowling came to a crossroads in life when her short-lived marriage fell apart, making her a single parent. During that time, she was barely surviving at the poverty level and just shy of becoming homeless. Dealing with that very dark period in her life, J.K. turned it around by focusing all her attention on finishing the only work that mattered to her. Rowling used rock bottom as a platform to relaunch her life.

Most individuals would agree with Rowling; failing is part of life. There is an upside to dealing with failure, as explained by Dr. Charles C. Manz in his book, *The Power of Failure,* Manz contends we must wrap our minds around a new definition. The Chaired Professor of Business Leadership at the University of Massachusetts sees failure as the "Short-termed unexpected results reflecting a challenge in progress." He professes failure provides three positive aspects: "A stepping stone to success, the opportunity for learning and development, and an opportunity for creative change and innovation."

Something about a new spin on the failure concept appeals to me. Viewing the experience not as an ending but "...a challenge in progress" makes it less of a pitfall and more like a hiccup. By adopting Manz's premise, we can embrace the learning lessons inherent in failure.

During my formative years, my mother, the eternal optimist, consistently doled out positive advice. She chirped in her Pollyanna style, "If at first, you don't succeed, try, try, try again." Sound familiar? No doubt, you heard that at home too. Thanks to some help from my mom, I learned early in life to avoid negative thinking patterns.

Ready to view failure from a different perspective? Next time you hit an obstacle on the path to success, look at it as a mere speed bump, just a temporary detour to the finish line. Change your failure definition, keep focused, and remember those four words taught to you as a child try, try, try again.

# Bitten By Atychiphobia

AS A CAREER COUNSELOR, I do a considerable amount of coaching on facing fear. Recently I accepted a new, rather complex project causing me to practice some heavy-duty self-coaching. I am not immune to driving myself "a bit nuts" over looming deadlines, key presentations, and, most importantly, the overall thought of screwing-up and failing. There is a word for the latter. Atychiphobia is a technical term for fear of failure, and sometimes that phobia has its way with us.

Atychiphobia can deter me from trying scary new things. I admit fear causes me to drag my feet. Once I've accepted the challenge, those emotional enemies in my head, I refer to as gremlins, often bombard me with self-doubt thoughts. Whenever I allow those gremlins control, anxiety sets in taking the form of a sleepless night that morphs into a nightmare depicting me in the starring role. Often in such a dream, I'm trying to get to an important meeting but continually get deterred by multiple roadblocks.

Stress and fear are cozy bed partners, so it is not uncommon to experience anxiety when confronted with a new challenge, but at some point, you need to face the unknown and take your power back. Becoming stress-hardy is doable; it just requires practicing some helpful techniques.

John Madison, a leadership guru, and author of the best-seller, *Real Leadership: 9 Simple Practices for Leading and Living with Purpose,* recommends separating the rational from the irrational. It makes sense, as we all tend to exaggerate our fears. Madison advises examining those disturbing thoughts to determine if they are truly rooted in reality.

When my anxiety level rose, I took John's advice and reviewed my concerns about failing in this project. He was spot-on. Most of my anxiety was inflated. After processing the overblown fear, I felt a sense of peace and renewed strength.

Another way to deal with an intimidating challenge is to review your many accomplishments. Often I advise clients to take stock of the positives before heading out to an interview. Positioning your value and worth in the forefront does much to diminish any thoughts of self-doubt.

You can also battle your trepidation with visualization. Spend a few minutes creating an image of how success will look and feel. Setting your thoughts on the outcome drives the doubts away.

Here's one final thought about overcoming fear of failure. Ever fail before? Well, this might sound counter-intuitive, but think about a past shortfall. Your world did not completely crumble, right? Sometimes, all it takes to drown out our inner critic's negative voice is to recognize failure is not the bogeyman. It's the thought of failing that brings us down. Use the strategies listed above, and failure will fade into the past, not become part of your present.

# Get Comfortable Being Uncomfortable

THE OTHER DAY THE FOLLOWING client email crossed my desk: "Sunny...I am spending a few days in Orlando enjoying my favorite theme park. Yesterday I waited patiently in line to board a roller coaster--which is something I never do! My purpose was to execute one of the items on my "Facing My Fears," list, which I created after our coaching session.

As they strapped me in, I took a deep breath. Closing my eyes, I said a quick prayer. As I was instantly plunged into the air at a frightening speed, you were the last image I remember before beginning the terrifying journey. At the end of the ride, I was happy to survive and thrilled with myself for dealing with the unknown."

I laughed heartily and applauded my client for stepping far afield of her comfort zone to deal with fear. Then I added, "take a roller coaster ride at the next opportunity" to my fear list. It is something I haven't done in years. Perhaps I lack the courage.

Dealing with fears holding us back from accomplishing our goals is a common theme in coaching sessions. My client mapping out a list of her worries was a proper beginning. Riding a roller coaster had nothing to do with her goals; however, conquering any fear, gives us the confidence to maintain momentum. Her closing sentence evidenced this, "I'm off to face my next fear."

Want to work on eliminating your barriers? Recognize that fears form in our minds. We associate doing something with danger, or perhaps we view the outcome as ending in embarrassment, disgrace, failure, etc.

Begin by striving to eliminate the negative and debilitating chatter in your head. It serves no purpose other than to provide excuses as worthless as a mechanical pencil devoid of lead. When those noisy demons begin their chant dismiss them. With no audience to entertain, they will quietly exit stage left.

Next, practice embracing uncertainty. Begin taking small risks consistently. Select activities that will help you conquer your fear. For example, if you fear public speaking, enroll in a Toastmasters class. The Toastmaster environment is supportive, allowing a participant to move at his or her own pace.

A final thought...borrow a tagline from the Navy Seals. "Get comfortable being uncomfortable." The idea is to remain focused on the task at hand regardless of the surrounding circumstances. Conditions will not always be ideal. Accept that fact and stay the course.

Feeling more secure about taking the plunge? Great! Meet me at Disneyland. I have a coaster to conquer.

# The Grind

THIS MORNING I MET WITH my client, Justin, who is on the cusp of something exciting, but at the same time terrified, he will fail. Some coaches might advise he invite fear into his life, embrace it, and work through it. I'm not part of that fear camp. Wasting precious energy dealing with anxiety won't get the job done.

There is no denying fear of failure is natural, but if we give into spending time listening to those scary gremlins in our heads, we divert our attention from taking actions that result in success. During my discussion with Justin, I recommended a few strategies that help blast away cynical fear-mongering.

Like most mid-careerists, my 45-year-old client experienced many triumphs in life. Why not spend time revisiting those victories. To achieve former goals, Justin tapped into his inner strength. He knows there is no simple formula for success. Grinding through the rough spots, and working harder than the rest of the tribe got him to the goal line in the past. Justin smiled in agreement when I reminded him that he and hard work are not strangers.

My client also revealed that others lean on him for strength. I responded there are seasons in life we must respect, however now is not the time to take on the project of helping other individuals deal with their issues. Then, with a little tough love, I quoted award-winning author, Mo Willems, "If you ever find yourself in the wrong story, leave."

Converting Justin's business concept into a viable, successful entity takes laser focus. Out-grinding the competition leaves no room for diversion or allowing others to zap your strength. Using the phrase "going underground" helped my client realize he need not be all things to all people. It is not selfish to spend the bulk of your time on your own goals. Once he experiences the big win, he can take a time out, and gracefully utilize his leisure time as a Good Samaritan.

Lastly, my advice was filling the day with continuous movement directed on his singular goal. We both had a good laugh over that one. Discipline is his middle name, so action is never a struggle. Justin hits the gym every morning like a gladiator. Having a solid workout under his belt gives him the confidence to leap fearlessly, embrace the rhythm of living in the moment, and get the job done.

How about you? Ready to toss fear aside and move your mountain? If the answer is yes, get in the starting blocks. Accept the fact that it's going to be a grind, requiring dedication and tremendous effort. Once you're focused on working hard, you won't have time to entertain thoughts of failure.

# Fear

In Summary:

- Take your power back
- Visualize success
- Own your mistake
- Create a do-over
- Eliminate excuses
- Use what you have
- Avoid negative thinking patterns
- Embrace uncertainty
- Deal with challenges
- Exit the wrong story
- Move your mountain

# Change Management Dealing with Transition

"It may be hard for an egg to turn into a
bird: it would be a jolly sight harder for it to
learn to fly while remaining an egg."

— C. S. Lewis

# An Inscription Worth Remembering

THE OTHER DAY I CONNECTED with my friend LaDonna who told me about a ring she wears daily inscribed with the words "Siempre Adelante," which means always forward. The ring reminds her to "accept life's inevitable disappointments and changes." Indeed, a lesson worth remembering. Inspired, I created a "Siempre Adelante" sign and hung it on my vision board.

LaDonna's communication contained two essential concepts. First, be mindful of the fact that from time to time, trouble is going to waltz through our lives uninvited. Life excels at either keeping us on our toes or knocking us totally off balance. We get comfortable cruising along experiencing smooth sailing, and then an unexpected wave of trouble churns the still waters. You know the drill. Disappointment, stress, and even a bit of panic occurs when the wind blows our sails in the wrong direction. It's normal to feel as deflated as a rapidly leaking lifeboat. But then what?

My first piece of advice is, don't bury your head in the sand. Spending time in denial is futile. There is a quote attributed to Elvis Presley putting setbacks in perspective. "Truth is like the sun. You can shut it out for a time, but it ain't going way." Accept the reality of the situation. The fact is, it happened, it's real, and it requires a solution.

Here's another scenario to avoid. I know it's tempting, but don't let your emotions rule. Wallowing in anger, worry, and self-pity only serves to zap your energy reserves. Spending time doing the "poor me" moan to anyone with a listening ear is time wasted. Whatever it is, a speeding ticket, a broken relationship, a job loss, or an unfortunate investment, take action and attack the problem. Need help on where to begin? Try rewinding a bit, and take comfort in the past. Undoubtedly you have faced downturns before and found a way to soldier on. Once you have regained your confidence, get focused, and tap into your creativity. Start brainstorming a way to get back in the game.

The second concept in the inscribed phrase pushes us into the future. Just as you can rewind to past achievements, you can fast-forward to brighter times. Take a breath and imagine your relief when you've solved the problem. Next, build up some momentum by putting one foot in front of the other and work your action plan. Where will that take you? In the right direction, always forward!

# Sometimes You Feel Like a Hotdog

WHILE TAKING IN THE SIGHTS on the Las Vegas strip, I suddenly realized I was famished. We were in Caesar's Palace, so I suggested we head over to Chef Bobby Flay's Mesa Grill. When I thought about the Blue Corn Pancake and Barbeque Duck entrée on the lunch menu, my mouth watered. Unfortunately, my taste buds were in for a disappointment. We missed lunch a la Flay due to hours of sightseeing.

My Plan B was heading toward an adjacent food court in search of something healthy, while my husband selected an all-American vendor who served hot dogs and beer. Snagging a table, I sat down with my salad. My spouse took a seat, relating a story about the man in front of him who placed an order. The clerk identified the customer as the chef of a local high-end restaurant. She was delighted to have him at her food stand but puzzled. When she questioned him, the chef shrugged his shoulders and replied with a smile, "Sometimes you just feel like a hot dog."

I love that story because it smacks of simplicity. We often over-complicate our lives. Some of us need to clear the decks and make some changes if we intend to simplify. For example, some of my clients are slaves to technology. During our sessions, they obey my rule and turn off their smartphones with a sigh of relief. I get the feeling it is one of the few times those phones ever go dark. Our high tech toys can both streamline and complicate our lives. It is perfectly acceptable to "unplug," withdraw from all communication modes and enjoy some tranquility.

Taking it down a notch is not just about managing your work hours. Are you a slave to your social calendar? Do you feel obligated to spend time with people when you'd rather be home working on a hobby or spending time with your family? Understand this, "no" is a powerful two-letter word that can put you in control. If jazz is not your preference and the gang is off to hear some band jamming Coltrane's work, politely opt-out. If a cynical friend habitually bends your ear for hours about all the drama in her life, find a way to distance yourself. Perhaps it's your commute that takes hours out of your life? Consider a move or look for a new job.

And finally, if throwing dinner parties for friends causes stress and involves an excessive amount of time in the kitchen, simplify the menu, or suggest potluck. If all else fails, just serve hot dogs with a dollop of mustard and lots of love.

# Retooling for Change

GRABBING A MAGAZINE, I MADE my way out the door. The waiting room would be an ideal time to catch up on reading one of the many periodicals delivered to my door. Full disclosure, I had to force myself to select this particular magazine. I hadn't read any of the issues in months, and I knew why. The publication converted from a typical shiny cover to a stock parchment with a different look and feel. Even the pages between the cover had lost their luster.

As I began leafing through the magazine searching for an interesting article, I soon settled on one about an editor who wrote about attempting to conquer her biggest fear: performing stand-up comedy. By the time I got to the third paragraph, I had forgotten all about the tactical feel I had missed. After reading three articles in the time allotted, I came to a conclusion. When I stopped to think about the untouched back issues piling up in my office, I realized I was avoiding change. Something that was no longer shiny, smooth, and familiar was left ignored because it was different. Shame on me a so-called change agent!

This revelation caused me to examine some other areas of my life. Running through my memory bank, I wondered, did I always drive the same route, hang out with the same friends, and frequent the same restaurants? Had I stopped searching out the new and different? At the end of my reverie, I came up somewhat guilty as charged. I sighed and vowed to start shaking things up in my everyday life.

Why do we avoid change? The answer is easy. It takes energy and means removing ourselves from auto-pilot. I've read enough books about changing habits to know the limbic part of our brain doesn't like change and would be blissfully happy to do the same things over and over again.

Want to change something in your life? Here's the good news. There are only three parts to implementing change: desire, intent, and persistence. You must do the work; it doesn't happen on its own. Be like the editor who changed her behavior and ended up on an improv stage in a Dallas comedy house. Okay, perhaps stand-up isn't your game, but you can experience and accomplish something new and different. When you do, your life will become more interesting. Don't try, do. I did.

# In the Words of Eleanor

THE OTHER NIGHT I WAS a guest at a dinner party given by a friend. A diverse group of interesting women attended. At one point during the evening, we discussed the impact of making life changes. A lively dialogue ensued, leaving me with many valuable takeaways. One of the comments that resonated with me came from Stacey, a licensed physical therapist.

While treating stroke patients, Stacy explained that she is not doing her job if they are comfortable in their therapy. She added, "For the brain to recover, to build new pathways, we have to stretch ourselves outside our comfort zone and experience new things."

Stacy shared how she applies that philosophy to her everyday living. "If you're feeling comfortable with your life and your career, change it up. We are only growing when we're uncomfortable." Each day she challenges herself to step outside of the box, no matter how scary or loud her inner voice begs her not to. Stacy believes in the words of Eleanor Roosevelt, who urged us to "Do one thing every day that scares you."

Eleanor is an admirable role model for many women. In her memoir *My Year with Eleanor*, Noelle Hancock gains the courage to face difficult growth challenges daily by studying the life of the former First Lady. After doing so, the author committed 365 days to follow Eleanor's wise counsel to embrace challenges and overcome her fears.

Think about it. Whether it is challenging a minor fear daily or a monster fear over time, the key to accomplishing tasks means having the guts to do it. Take a look at the list of goals you created for this year. Are any missing? Perhaps it's what you would like to accomplish most but are just too darn chicken to attempt.

Try rethinking the goal with an if/then scenario. For example, years ago, I wanted to carve out a successful corporate career. The only thing preventing success was my fear of public speaking. Rising through the ranks meant having the courage to face a group of two or two-hundred or more. My if/then proposal went like this: If I conquer my fear of public speaking, then I will be able to grow my career. Wanting it badly enough prompted me to enroll in a Dale Carnegie course. Still no easy feat, I repeated the program twice to make sure I would no longer tremble with knees knocking when asked to present to an audience.

What's holding you back? Commit to looking fear in the face and staring it down. As Stacy so aptly advised, if you are comfortable, you are not growing.

# Get Out of The Zone

As a career coach, I am a change agent who teaches others to embrace transformation. Taking internal stock over the past week, I found myself falling into the Cobbler's Children Syndrome. You remember the shoemaker who was so busy making shoes for the townspeople his children went shoeless. Well, color me shoe-less, but not clueless.

Here's the deal. I've allowed myself to sink into my comfort zone, which happened gradually and without warning. One day you wake up and realize nothing is changing. Living in that comfy routinized sector is so alluring. Everything is familiar with no threat of risk or challenge. In the zone, you maintain a low-stress level, relatively free of anxiety. Do not be deceived! That is not a good thing. Even my dog recognizes the need for change. Sure, Zoli has his favorite napping places, but to my amazement, he continues to find new and different areas of our home for an afternoon siesta.

Think of your comfort zone like visiting your parent's home. You can rest there for a while, but you cannot live there. If you ever tried returning to the nest, you know what I mean. The reason parenting birds push their offspring out of that cozy feathered shell is so they can fly.

Need to bust out of the nest? Commit to making changes. It's okay to start small. One of the co-authors of *The 52 Weeks: How Two Women Got Unstuck, Got Inspired, and Got Going,* began by simply incorporating blueberries into her daily diet. From there, she branched out into trying a new challenge every week during the year. She became a change artist who tried everything from learning the art of poker to taking weekly tango lessons.

Don't over-think it. Just do it. Right now, take the next ninety seconds to conjure up the change you will incorporate into your life this week. Are you on a roll now? Excellent! Make a list of things that exist in your "someday I will" fantasy and key it into your calendar now. Long ago, I learned nothing happens unless it is firmly planted into your schedule. Crank up your excitement level by mapping it out into days, weeks, and months.

Are you feeling fearful of change? That's normal. What if you don't like skydiving? Fine, don't continue jumping out of planes, but kudos to you for venturing out. You gave your brain a boost. Now put away your adult coloring book, strap on your dancing shoes, and tap your way to a more exciting life.

# Like a Hermit Crab

JAMIE ARRIVED AT MY OFFICE, looking like sleep eluded her. Observing the dark circles beneath her soft brown eyes signaled me; she was dealing with a stressful situation. Jamie shared her dilemma. She had arrived at a crossroad and was struggling with which path to take.

My client had a decision to make regarding her career life. Typically any issue with your profession tends to spill into your non-work life. Since this business scenario involved relocation, Jamie had more to consider than a straight-forward promotion.

She needed a decision process that would result in a clear, confident choice. When I inquired regarding the number one reason keeping her awake at night, Jamie admitted it was fear of the unknown. I nodded my head in understanding. Whenever we consider stepping out of that cushy comfort zone we live in, our inner gremlins, dwelling in the status-quo, jump up and down calling foul.

It helped Jamie to understand fear is a natural part of the process. If only we could be as comfortable with change as a hermit crab. This nocturnal crustacean lives in a shell until she outgrows it. Whether it's with ease, or trepidation, Ms. Crab ventures out of the confining space and scurries along the ocean floor searching for a larger new home, repeating this process throughout her life. Jamie admitted that if a palm-sized crab could depart from her comfort zone and deal with the temporary uneasiness of changing conditions, so could she.

Before we can make a decision, we must have all the facts at hand. As we sorted through Jamie's relocation package, she made a list of three areas requiring clarification. Things looked a bit brighter as we discussed the short and long-term impacts on her family if she forged ahead with the promotion. Jamie assigned a value rating to each benefit. By the time she finished a list of action items, I could see a change in her body language; she was beginning to relax.

As our session ended, Jamie agreed to gather any missing information. My final caution was "sleep on it," which is my go-to remedy for just about everything. Back-burnering, an issue for 24 hours, helps clear our minds. Studies prove sleep organizes our memories, processes information, and aids in decision-making.

Try enlisting those simple techniques to help you make an informed decision next time you're standing at a crossroads. It could be a small leap or a large one, but whatever you decide, emerge from your shell and do it with confidence.

# Word of The Year

My friend Jeanette sent me an article by philanthropist Melinda Gates, who, rather than making resolutions for the new year, chooses a word of the year that encapsulates her aspirations for the next twelve months. After soaking up her wise thoughts, I decided to follow suit and select a word or phrase that I could use as a mantra to, as Melinda expressed it, "Make the year better and make me better."

As I contemplated selecting a phrase to inspire me throughout the year, I glanced down at my desktop. Sitting in one corner, I spied two quarters, a nickel and a bright shiny penny. I had to laugh, wondering if it could be any more obvious. My mantra for this year is change-agent!

You know there are some years, like Melinda's 2016, when your word should be gentle, as a reminder to go easy on yourself and stop striving for perfection. Not this year! If like me, you are ready to make some major changes, then read along, I have some suggestions.

Let me begin with some tough love. Embrace failure. That's right. If you're going to make some mega-sized changes in your life, you might, at some point, get thrown on your backside. Prepare yourself for this and push back. If you fall, go down swinging, and don't let it discourage you. Get tough, be resilient, and deal with it, then try another approach. Next, get comfortable being uncomfortable. Your actions over the next 12 months will take you far from the safe zone.

Now that you've primed your courage muscles, forget giant leaps, and act as a bricklayer. Take one action at a time, and keep making progress. In the classic Aesop's Fable tale, the arrogant hare lost because he stopped to nap along the way. Emulate the tortoise, slow and steady wins the race.

Ready to team up with other change-agents? You can start by reading. Life coach, M.J. Ryan wrote one of my favorite books on change: *This Year I Will.* The coach lays out ten tips for making change and offers up powerful techniques to keep you moving forward without throwing in the towel.

Are you feeling motivated? Forget the someday I will pipe dreams and get ready to tackle the year ahead. Make this your year of change. Show up with grit and determination. Acknowledge you are serious and committed. If you do, you will look back on the year with immense pride.

Now, come on, let's roll! Make each step count just like our friend the tortoise.

# A Powerful Life Tool

WHEN I WANT TO CONVEY an important message, I prefer doing it in writing. Why? Because before I press that non-forgiving send button, I can edit away, again and again, until the blank screen fills with the perfect tone and concise statements. Reviewing each word, phrase, and punctuation mark help me get my point across precisely as I intended.

Editing is a fantastic tool designed not solely for adjusting words on a document. Why not edit your life? There are parts of my life, and probably yours that can be removed to make room for more meaningful activities.

Let's begin with people. Do you have friendships that are weighing you down? From time to time, an individual appears on the horizon that does all the taking. Know anyone like that? Put bluntly; your fake friend is a narcissist. You find yourself dancing to the beat of her drum while your personal goals and priorities evaporate, right? Here's some tough love. You cannot have a healthy relationship with someone so self-involved, so exit that person out stage left and make room for more meaningful and balanced friendships.

Think about editing other areas of existence. Any chance you make yourself nuts striving for perfection? I've found aiming for the perfect this or the ideal that is like chasing an elusive moving target. For example, have the dinner parties you create become so complicated you find yourself stressing over each minute detail? If so, call yourself out on that. Yes, I get it. I, too, am heavily influenced by The Food Channel; however, we are not all meant to carry off an elaborate meal, ala Martha Stewart. Relax and calm down. Forget trying to duplicate Gordon Ramsey's signature Beef Wellington dish and grill up a mean hamburger. Your friends will be happy with a side of potato salad and your company.

What else is nonessential in your life? Are you spending too much time on social media? That can be one mega timesuck. It's okay to be social and connect with others on Facebook, LinkedIn, and Instagram but consider exercising some discipline. Give yourself a time limit. My rule is 15 minutes once per day. That should allow adequate time to send out birthday wishes and see what's going on with your old college roommate.

Are there things in your life taking up too much space? My downfall was magazines. I love glossy pages filled with articles and succumbed to subscribing to numerous publications. Edit out your overconsumption.

This week take a bird's-eye view of your life and make some changes. Decide what to keep and then let go of the unnecessary time wasters. With careful editing, I promise the result is an uncomplicated life that brings you more joy and peace.

# Change Management

- Edit your life
- Always forward
- Have a Plan B
- Simplify your desires
- Commit to changes
- Don't over think it
- Step outside the box
- Sleep on it
- Emerge from your shell
- Get a mentor
- Do the work
- Embrace failure

# Lessons Learned
# Drink in Experience

"You don't learn to walk by following the rules.
You learn by doing, and by falling over."

— RICHARD BRANSON

# Stumbles and Screw-Ups

WHEN I ASKED MY NEW client, Josh, his goals for our coaching sessions, without missing a beat, he responded that he wanted his life to be a complete do-over. Whoa! Thinking it was a bit drastic, I smiled and suggested he imagine using a large Wite-Out Correction Pen to ink out the mistakes, but only after reviewing the outcome and internalized lessons learned.

Let's face facts. We all suffer stumbles and screw-ups. Understandably, marching down memory lane and recalling our regrets is painful. But before kicking all the failures to the curb, it is necessary to capture the knowledge gained. There is truth in the expression that our best teacher is our biggest blunder. Why? We often learn best when digging out of our deepest holes.

Ready to do this? First, keep in mind that you've already made the mistake. Having suffered the consequences, you may as well extract the lesson. Analyzing errors helps us find out what works and what doesn't. Absorbing the cost of our wayward ways promotes corrective action and change, which eventually leads to success.

Want more reasons to put our mess-ups under the microscope? Mistakes enhance our skill level. To err is human, but an astute individual never repeats the same blunder. In the aftermath of a regrettable experience, we walk away wiser human beings. Failures reveal our blind spots. We learn a great deal from a thorough inspection of our faux pas. This insight helps us grow. Writer and motivational speaker Denis Waitley bottom-lined it when he stated, "There are no mistakes or failures, only lessons."

A word of caution here. While you are processing the lessons, don't be too hard on yourself. No one handed you a road map to your life's journey. Executing is sometimes a crapshoot, so we are forced to take risks. Expecting to get it right, 100% of the time is unrealistic.

Upon returning for a follow-up session, Josh and I discussed the valuable insight gained from his soul-searching error assessment. Admitting it was a worthwhile exercise; he was now poised to put the past behind him and move forward. After rewinding some of the rough terrains he experienced, Josh expressed confidence about taking an alternate path with a newfound awareness of the pitfalls. Rather than continually going it alone, he vowed to also reach out for help when needed.

Will he mess up again? Will I? Will you? Of course! To think we'll never make another mistake ever again is unrealistic. But as a wise man once said, the only real mistake is one from which we learn nothing.

# Running on Empty

As I DROVE AROUND TOWN running errands, my car signaled to me with a soft dinging sound. Initially, I didn't know what my car was indicating. Before long it dawned on me, I was low on gas. Usually, my considerate husband keeps my tank full so, it was the first time I heard the warning alert.

Smart cars and phones conveniently tell us when things need refueling or recharging. Using this analogy, listen to your inner voice, and you will discover your internal dashboard also provides warning signs. It sends off a signal when we are, as singer-songwriter Jackson Browne put it, "running on empty."

Stopping to refresh and renew is vital to our physical and emotional wellbeing. Recently a client told me she was so fed up and discouraged with her job search she came up with a counter-intuitive action plan. Rather than turn up the fire on job-related activities, she pulled the plug, deciding she needed a change of scenery. Unemployment provided an opportunity to visit an emotionally supportive family who lived out-of-state.

Ceci packed up the car with a suitcase, her favorite music, Cinnamon, her faithful dog, and hit the road. As she traveled, delighted aunts and uncles offered all the love and nurturing needed to recharge. By the time she returned home, my client felt renewed and ready to jump back into finding a position to add value and use her skills. Before long, she was scheduling interviews with companies on her target list.

Okay, I get it. Not all unemployed individuals can embark on a road trip. And not all burn out is related to employment issues. But the lesson learned here is, no matter how busy you think you are, step aside when you're spinning your wheels and near hitting the wall. When frustration accelerates into unhealthy stress, like a GPS, your warning bell will sound loud and clear. Do not ignore it! Stop running on empty and refuel your emotional tank by calling a time out.

Consider your options. How about a day trip to the spa, an early morning hike, or a bike ride to the beach or nature center? You may find it best to spend quiet time alone, or perhaps the perfect prescription for your situation is surrounding yourself with your A-team's caring people.

Whatever your go-to remedy is, utilize it. Once you enjoy some downtime, a change of scenery, or the warmth of your loved ones, you'll gain the energy to get back in action and take your best shot.

# When Does the
# Party End?

ONE DAY WHILE LISTENING TO a podcast, I found myself in utter awe of Darren Hardy, the presenter, as he spoke about a personal pity party. We throw one when we suffer a disappointment that knocks us on our keister, making us want to crawl under the covers with a bowl of fudge brownie ice cream and never resurface. Okay, I'm not referencing serious tragedies here. It's more like losing a significant contract you thought was a slam-dunk, or receiving the twenty-seventh rejection letter on your book or getting the "I think we should see other people," AKA break-up call.

Darren said he whittled down wallowing-in-sorrow from two weeks to two days, two hours, to two minutes or back up to twenty minutes if it is a colossal setback.

The pity party subject frequently comes into play during a client's coaching session. I'm a bit more lenient than Darren. My standard advice is to limit the "woe is me scenario" to 24 hours. Let yourself feel the pain, lick your wounds then get right back up.

Real estate mogul Barbara Corcoran, who annually invests $1.75 million on the hit show "Shark Tank," says this is about the bounce-back factor. The Real Estate tycoon takes a chance on an individual only if her gut tells her the entrepreneur possesses the ability to get hurt and quickly recover.

How can you step-up your bounce-back rate? First, recognize your negative emotions. Understandably you're hurting. It is okay to experience those feelings. Next, get active. Try writing about it, vent away on your keyboard, or paper! Put out the stops and play some loud heavy rock music as you pound out your venom.

Feeling better? Time to move on and access the damages. Dig deep. Did you play any role in causing the upset, or was it totally beyond your control? Ask yourself what you could have done differently to skew the outcome. Making notes on lessons learned helps the healing process.

Lastly, focus on something positive. If you have not quite recovered from your funk using my outlined method, go directly to the freezer and pull out the Cherry Garcia or whatever flavor puts a smile on your face. Avoid jumping under the covers. Instead, dial in a funny video and lose yourself in laughter.

Realistically, some of us may never match a two-minute sulk and recovery, but it is possible to skinny down the time we spend singing the blues. Keep working at it. There may be a day when you stand before Corcoran and the rest of the Sharks. Show them you are a winner who can rapidly bounce back!

# No Matter What

EVER FIND YOURSELF IN A motivational slump? Last week as I viewed large pockets of free time on my calendar, I was practically doing backflips thinking of the precious hours I could spend advancing on my goals. It turns out; it didn't happen that way. What occurred was a total lack of motivation, followed by frittering the hours away, ending in zero progress.

Determined not to let this happen again, I resorted to research. Needing stimulation beyond my self-coaching, I scanned through some motivational blogs and came up short. Everything read like the same old blah, blah, blah that ran through my head. Nothing signaled a brain spark until I noticed a post by Olympic athlete, Inga Stasiulionyte. Now I was onto something. If anyone could help me carve a path out of this listless do-nothing fog, a javelin thrower turned executive coach had a chance. Anyone who followed her dream to the Beijing Olympic Games knows something about victory.

As I studied her approach to success, it all boiled down to discipline. Okay, nothing new, we all know it takes commitment and focus; however, in this simple sentence, Inga offered up a key to get me back on track. "Build a no-matter-what mindset." Aha! You see all week long I gave myself permission to goof-off. I decided if I could permit a lax attitude, I could also create a no-matter-what mindset.

While testing it out the next day, I encountered some resistance. After working on my top priority for thirty minutes, I found myself eating a fudge bar while cleaning out a desk drawer. My brain preferred to operate on autopilot and wasn't buying into this new mindset thing. Faced with the choice of rearranging my desk or returning to work, I vacillated for a moment. As I surveyed the objects in the drawer, I spied a big black marker. Grabbing the fat pen and a sheet of paper, I wrote in large block letters "no matter what" and stuck it on the wall in front of me. Eyeing that powerful phrase was what I needed to kick me back into action.

This new mindset worked again the next day. You see, I live in the desert and was late getting out for my power walk. Feeling like the heat was getting to me, I considered cutting my trek short. Taking a deep breath, I looked up at the sun and proclaimed (yep...you guessed it) no matter what! It was all I needed to suck it up and finish my walk.

Let's face it. Human beings fall into slumps that thwart progress. When the doldrums take over, search out a role model who didn't give up. Grab on to a motivational mantra and push yourself forward. Although I cannot correctly pronounce Inga's last name, I assure you I will never forget her for inspiring a "no-matter-what" mindset. Game on!

# Beating Down
# the Gophers

THORNY EXPERIENCES ARE CHALLENGING. BRUISED memories from a taxing ordeal tend to linger on like a bad dream. Emotional baggage not only casts a negative shadow, but it also takes up space. Living with a past hurt is like having a dark dungeon-like living room crammed full of unsightly objects that bar you from opening a window to let in the sunshine.

Ridding yourself of the urge to ruminate over past hurts might take some extra effort, maybe even some pageantry or radical action. Recently I read about a practice called a sorrow bonfire. I never was a Campfire Girl, but the idea appeals to me. There is power in fire. Take your painful experience and commit it to paper. Trek out to the beach or a campsite and create a bonfire. You might even bring friends along to witness the event. With sincere reflection, toss your missive in the fire. As you watch the document go up in flames, reflect on the fact it's been reduced to ash and can no longer throw a dark pallor over your life.

Sometimes you need to beat the crap out of a huge hurt. Years ago, when I felt my stress and frustration level mounting,

I would head out to a local fun zone and make a beeline for a game involving a soft mallet to beat down pop-up gophers. Smacking those little guys back in their hole was not only a fun stress reliever; I also racked up multiple valuable redeemable points. My next move was to gift some little person with tickets to use at the prize exchange. In return, the smiles I received were worth all the money I poured into the gopher machine and left me with a content feeling on the drive home.

In her book, *Happiness as a Second Language,* author Valerie Alexander offers up another action to rid yourself of a painful experience. Fill a piñata with fun little treats. Next, hang it up and hammer your paper-mache character with all your might as you commit to letting go of the bad memory forever. Then scoop up the delights and share them with others.

Ready to leave your pain behind and move on? Try the bonfire or piñata or any other method that ends in joy. Let go of the hurt. It's time.

# Sometimes You Must Say Uncle

I JUST RETURNED FROM A girlfriends' getaway weekend. It was a delightful time spent shopping, sightseeing, and swapping life experiences. We often lingered over lattes or evening cocktails catching up on the latest news involving careers, families, and mutual friends. Over the years, the four of us developed a sterling bond and mutual respect. As our friendships run deep, it is common during the time spent together to share dreams, reveal fears, and solicit opinions for honest feedback.

One afternoon Donna related a recent life lesson. Her husband, a motorcycle enthusiast, encouraged her to share his passion and surprised her by having a new Harley-Davidson delivered to their home. Within days Donna had her first riding lesson and was licensed to operate a motorcycle.

My friend is an adventurous gutsy woman who loves life and outdoor activities. She is an expert skier, a certified scuba diver, and an avid hiker.

Although Donna adores spending time with her husband Jake, a problem arose when she discovered their joint motorcycling outings were far from what she expected. After enduring each ride on a white-knuckle basis, she felt physically ill from stress. My friend is no cream puff. As a positive thinker, she envisioned her fear and anxiety diminishing. However, the angst only increased. Eventually, she felt forced to make a tough decision. The sport was not for her, and this meant quitting.

Her story holds a much-overlooked life lesson. Many of us are so focused on being winners. Repeatedly we use mantras like "failure is not an option," to pump ourselves up. In my coaching practice, I encourage clients to face and conquer their fears. But Donna's motorcycle story stopped me in my tracks. It made me realize that sometimes the prize is just not worth the effort. Quitting when it doesn't feel right does not make us any less of a winner. Sometimes the wisest course of action is to call out uncle and hang up our helmet.

The moral of the story is we do not have to climb every mountain put in front of us. There are times when the prudent thing to do is go around it or turn back and take a different path. One final thought, when opting out of a challenge, do not label it defeat. Chin up, move on and do so with dignity.

# Down in The Details

STEVEN ENTERED MY OFFICE, ANNOUNCING he was on the count-down. Catching my puzzled expression, my client explained it was 19 days and counting until we could advance the calendar to a new year. Scowling, he admitted dreading all the upcoming holiday parties where friends and relatives would query how he fared during the year.

I realized Steven had some setbacks recently, but few of us experience the perfect 12 months where everything goes right, and all our dreams come true. Although he wanted to work with me on creating new goals for next year, I changed the game plan. It is essential to do a year in review and clear the decks before setting goals for the new year.

Determined not to let him dismiss the entire 365 days as a lost cause, I challenged him to recount small victories and hard-won lessons. First, I pressed Steven to relate one thing he accomplished that made him proud. After pondering the question for a few moments, I watched as a glimmer of satisfaction crossed his face. Steven told me about a new website he created for a client that significantly drove traffic, resulting in increased sales. Over the next few minutes, we drilled down on a few more triumphs worth a fist bump or two.

We cannot learn from our mistakes and leverage actions into valuable lessons if we don't get analytical. During the second part of this exercise, I asked Steven to review a failed situation with a critical yet objective lens. He cringed and indicated a discussion would be too painful, but I refused to give in. At that point, we discussed a complicated business situation, detailing ten key factors on my whiteboard as lessons learned.

After completing the exercise, Steven was ready to honor his holiday party commitments with a positive attitude. As I bid him a Happy New Year, his parting words were, "You know; it wasn't such a bad year after all."

How about it? Don't let a time period end without having a serious discussion with yourself or a trusted mentor. Before you can even commit to new goals and objectives, you must clear the slate. What worked? What didn't and why? No guilt allowed just clinical objectivity.

Once you have completed a looking back review, I believe, like Steven, you will greet the future feeling like a more prosperous, self-confident you. Acknowledge all your small victories and turn every ending into a positive beginning.

# Lessons Learned

In Summary:

- Flame out the hurt
- Use your objective lens
- Clear the slate
- Acknowledge victories
- Flex your discipline muscle
- Employ no matter what
- Heed your warning bell
- Know when to quit
- Analyze screw-ups
- Grow from insight
- Minimize the pity party

# Tenacity
# Stay The Course

"Tenacity is when you follow your heart, when the whole
word is screaming at you to get back into your head."

— Sonia Choquette

# The Champ, The Dumbbells and Me

ABOUT THREE HOURS INTO THE church breakfast, it dawned on me. I felt great. Generally, my volunteer job of cooking and scrubbing pots and pans would make me weary by this time. But today left me feeling I could do the lunch and dinner service too. With a knowing smile, I attributed my physical wellbeing to a strength training regimen I recently incorporated into my schedule. About six weeks ago, I employed a fitness trainer to help me build lean muscle and lose undesirable body fat. Now it became evident the discipline and determination were starting to pay off.

In the beginning, I was slightly skeptical about the workout sessions. There was nothing fun or sexy about pushing barbells up to my chin or spending time using dumbbells at multiple angles. Additionally, I had to learn a whole new vocabulary. I push myself focused on "two away from failure" while trying to remember from my college anatomy class where my deltoid muscles are and how to engage my biceps and triceps fully. At the same time, I need to count the reps and alternate the sets. This regiment was a whole new way to torture my mind and body, knowing the next morning I would experience aches in muscles I'd forgotten I owned.

I hung in there because the folks at the Mayo Clinic said strength training helps you preserve and enhance your muscle mass at any age. I learned as your body gains muscle, it burns calories more efficiently. I was all for pushing my body to assist me in that department. It also helped that my trainer lavished praise on me when I "held my form" or completed "a perfect set." (A little approval goes a long way with me.)

The most challenging part of upholding my fitness regimen was going to the gym alone. I had to commit my workouts in writing on my calendar. Each day I spent at least 30 minutes convincing myself of the importance of working out when I preferred to do something, anything else.

Setting goals is easy. Doing the work is hard, especially when the payoff is not immediate. We can all get very creative when it comes to rationalizing why we should slack off. What should you do when you feel like quitting? Stop your head chatter, and just do it. The Champ, Muhammad Ali, once admitted he "hated every minute of training." I figure if "The Greatest" can hate training, I can detest those darn dumbbells. Now, if anyone is looking for me, I'll be in the gym.

# Volley for Success

EVER LOSE STEAM TRYING TO accomplish your goals? I can relate. In fact, at times, individuals I coach come to sessions complaining of failure due to a lack of enthusiasm. It's not unusual to experience waning motivation. Getting back on track requires some introspection and perhaps some inspiration.

Recently I received a lesson in motivation from a 12-year-old. Ever watch a youth prepare for sports tryouts? I observed my pre-teen niece in competition for the volleyball team. Aisalynn is a self-motivated student who sets the bar high without any coaching from her parents. Her latest goal was to make the volleyball team.

Proper tools are required to accomplish any goal. As Aisalynn began the process, she realized essential equipment was needed. Exercising her independence, she solved this challenge by using her savings to purchase a volleyball and knee pads.

There was a learning curve involved. My niece was new to the tryout process and had never really played the sport. I watched as she took every step in stride. During a week of learning the game at school, she spent dedicated hours in the evening practicing her skills.

How are you progressing on your major goal? Using Aisalynn's story as an example, consider the question of ownership. Is this something you truly want to accomplish, or are you doing what someone else feels is in your best interest? If you are not committed and excited about the goal, you are wasting your time. My advice, scratch it from your list.

Another test of commitment is, what must you invest? Perhaps you are pining for a promotion but need to upgrade your skills to be a viable contender. If you are not willing to plunk down your hard-earned cash for self-development, your chances of success are nearly nil.

Beyond being invested in your goal mentally and financially, you can renew your motivation by creating a solid plan. In the words of Tom Landry, "Setting a goal is not the main thing. It is deciding how you will go about achieving it and staying with that plan." Aisalynn was committed to a daily plan, and her plan worked. She made the team.

Take another look at your action plan. Does it include milestones anchored with specific dates for completion? If not, make some tweaks to get back on track.

A final suggestion, utilize the tryout mentality for motivation. Invest in yourself, do the work, follow the plan, and you will never have to worry about making the team.

# Inspiration in a Tube

MY HUSBAND SIGHED AND WATCHED me with his "there she goes again" grin as I skillfully maneuvered another squeeze of toothpaste out of the flattened tube. Although I'm not a super frugal person, getting the last dab out of every container that finds its way into our household is a challenge I rise to meet.

As I press down hard, managing to anoint my brush with a final dab of a fresh mint fluoride-free paste promising to rid my teeth of plaque while whitening, I remembered a speech I heard in a staff meeting long ago. A passionate talk, given by a colleague, did much to inspire a leadership group facing some dim financial results. I do not remember his name, but I will never forget the essence of his message. It was about always being able to squeeze out what you need.

I often use the toothpaste analogy for inspiration. Whether you are running a marathon or burning the midnight oil trying to finish a critical report, if you push hard enough, you can find the extra steam required to complete the task at hand. Is bringing the last drop of energy to the surface an easy feat? No, it takes a hefty dose of grit and some substantial mental prodding. Stated differently, you must draw on your willpower.

Dictionary.com defines willpower as a noun meaning "the ability to control oneself and determine one's actions." Well, pardon me, Mr. Webster, but I think your definition is only half right. Staying the course when you question how to keep going involves the will to power-through (verb).

One way to keep going when you want to throw in the towel is what I call "channel-changing." Let's take running the marathon, or any physical activity as an example. If your harmful mental chatter pipes up trying to convince you that you'll never reach the finish line, forget the finish line and think about a motivating subject. Visualize the glass of cold water waiting for you and the joy of hugging your five-year-old when the race is over. I employ that strategy with my fitness trainer. When I'm ready to say uncle, and he calls for more reps, I conjure up an image of the new sundress I bought. No way can I rock that beautiful sky-blue outfit with flabby arms.

So, the next time you need to power-through an activity when your tank registers empty, change the channel and think of squeezing that tube of paste. I know you can do it!

# Developing Resilience

SOMETIMES I'VE WONDERED IF I'M a creampuff. You know, no hard exterior. Recently my tough girl barometer was tested, and I have a mean-looking black eye to prove it! It happened on our way to dinner when I tripped over an uneven patch of payment. I went down before my husband could catch me, and in horror, he watched my head bounce off the pavement. I hobbled back to our hotel room while my man administered first aid. John suggested I lie down to rest, and we order dinner in. I firmly declined the shrinking violet role and opted for dinner out.

Okay, not a massive example of resilience, but the accident prompted some reflection. The only control we have is the ability to respond to what life throws at us. Whether the challenges are significant or small, like my fall, they can be strength-building opportunities. My head was sore and kept reminding me how hard cement feels when your skull dances off it, but I was determined not to let it ruin our evening.

According to Dr. Zelana Montminy, author of the book, *21 Days to Resilience*, living with resilience is more than just bouncing back; it is about shifting our perceptions, changing our responses, experiencing real growth. Resilient people refuse to let adversity define them. And the good news is resilience is not entirely genetic. It is a skill we can develop.

Want to be more iron-clad? Begin with practicing flexibility. My friend, Carmen, recently broke her foot and was warned by her doctor to put no pressure on the foot for eight weeks. Refusing to allow this to inhibit her travel, Carmen rented a scooter-like vehicle. Her broken foot rests off the ground while her strong leg pushes, providing momentum to travel around her home, the mall, or wherever she wants.

Other recommended strategies to encourage resiliency are keeping a positive outlook, embrace change, and become a diligent problem solver. When an unwelcome event occurs, adopting a "why me" stance is of no use. Start brainstorming ways to deal with whatever curveball life pitched your way.

As I reached for a way to embrace the change in my appearance, I thought hiring a talented face painter to transform my black eye into high fashion designer art would be pretty cool. Since that was not the most practical solution, I settled for a heavy-duty concealer lessening the dark-eye effect.

Remember, like it or not, difficulties occur. Work on becoming more resilient so you can face those challenges head-on. Don't act like a creampuff, be a dragon-slayer!

# Three No's Get
# to a YES!

THERE ARE VARIOUS METHODS OF attacking a goal and bringing
it to fruition. One successful strategy is the "no exception rule."
My client, Leyla, is a perfect role model. By employing this philosophy, she maintains a total dedication to her weight loss goal.
Leyla is the only person I know who not only nixed the pumpkin
pie but left the Thanksgiving table after a modest meal of green
beans, a small salad, and a three-ounce serving of boneless, skin-
less turkey breast. In addition to strict adherence to a physician
monitored diet, regular coaching sessions to hold her accountable, and a moderate aquatic exercise program Leyla recently
joined a weekly support group. As I watch her pulling out all the
stops to reach the goal line, I'm rating her level of dedication an
eleven on a ten scale.

When I asked Leyla why this strategy worked when others
failed, she admitted to her all or nothing mentality. Before
establishing her weight loss goal, Leyla analyzed prior disappointments as she battled overeating. In the past, when she
veered off-course, she quickly forgave herself and tried reset-
ting. The problem arose when she readily cut herself slack at

weak moments, which seemingly began to occur on a more frequent basis. In a light-bulb moment, Leyla realized the only way
to achieve success was to implement a philosophy of no excuses,
no exceptions, and no days off for good behavior.

I think the good doctor would agree. In his book, *Excuses
Begone!* renowned author and speaker, the late Dr. Wayne Dyer,
advises us to cast away our built-in subconscious crutches. Dyer
maintains no excuses are worth defending.

To implement a "no excuses" approach, you must first believe
you can achieve your desired objective. Leyla knew she was
skilled at attaining anything if she wanted it badly enough. You
are no different. Take a trip down memory lane and recall your
past triumphs. You did it before, and you can do it again. Next,
wrap your mind around reality. Accomplishing a significant goal
is never easy. It's gonna take grit!

The final segment in this strategy is enlarging your vision.
Leyla knew the approach to success should be multi-faceted. She
took power over her food fixation by enlisting a support and
accountability team. Friends who were aware of her goal stood
on the sidelines, cheering her on.

Ready to power through a major challenge? Focus on the
three no's, and you'll get there. No exceptions, no excuses, and
no time off!

# Escalation is Always
# An Option

OVER LUNCH, MY FRIEND ELLEN related a story about spending three hours on the phone with the airlines trying to sort out a mishap involving an international ticket. Most of us might have given up after thirty minutes. Not Ellen. She was beyond persistent; she was tenacious.

Tenacity is a characteristic successful people possess that propels them to the top. According to Webster, "a person who never gives up and never stops trying," is tenacious. During Ellen's three-hour marathon situation, she called for escalation when an agent could not resolve the issue. After waiting 30 minutes for a supervisor to come to the line, the agent claimed her manager was unavailable. Realizing she was at an impasse with this particular employee, Ellen hung up and tried the 800 number again. Faced with a new agent and new excuse, she continued to press on and eventually connected with a wise, experienced airline supervisor who created a solution. Lesson learned here: When a tenacious person teams with a creative thinker, all things are possible.

Effort alone does not always equal success, strategy counts, as does grit. Author Margaret Halsey proclaims, "Bulldogs have been known to fall on their swords when confronted by my superior tenacity." Halsey honed her tenacity muscle and accomplished her goals by never backing down to a formidable opponent.

How tenacious are you? Think about the last time you failed at something. Was another party involved? Did you accept no for an answer? Perhaps you let the person off the hook too soon. When negotiating, a passive stance signals if pushed, you will back down. Although Ellen heard the "no" word multiple times, there was no giving in. She viewed it as a speed bump, not the end of the road. Maintaining a firm but courteous demeanor Ellen pressed on and on and on.

Another hint, authority depends on your perception. Each airline representative believed she was fully authorized to negate Ellen's request. My friend could have stopped after the initial call, but did not cave to the agent's power over her situation. Ellen knows escalation is always an option and continually requested a higher authority.

When you want a raise in pay, an opportunity to bid on a project or purchase your dream car at a price you can afford practice tenacity. Stand tall, dig your heels in, be patient, and don't take no for an answer.

# Swing for the Fences

SPRING IS MY FAVORITE SEASON. No, it's not about April showers or May flowers, I'm talking the start of major league baseball. All my life I've had a love affair with the game. Growing up in a large city suburb, I could walk down the street and hear the score of an evening game drifting from house to house. All season long neighbors relaxed on their front porches listening to radio announcers giving a play-by-play account of each inning's activity.

One of my youth highlights was collecting baseball trading cards packaged with the bonus slice of bubble gum, but nothing beat witnessing the live-action in the stadium. Whenever possible, I cashed in my allowance and purchased a seat in the bleachers.

It should probably come as no surprise that my first date with my husband took place at a baseball game. That fateful night when the Detroit Tigers battled the Oakland A's is one of my favorite memories. As the competition extended into extra innings, I consumed one ice-cold beer, two hot dogs, some peanuts, and coincidently fell completely in love with my date.

Baseball always brings out the optimist in me. Think about a tie game narrowed down to the bottom of the ninth with the bases loaded. The final pitch can end in a win, a loss, or a second chance for either team to make a comeback. It's like that in life. There are times when we feel the odds stack up against us. Frustrated, we know we could pull it off if we could catch a break. It's that second chance I find so alluring. Each new day is another opportunity to come from behind and knock one out of the ballpark.

Ever feel like you're the batboy rather than the staring slugger? You don't have to remain in that position. Shift your focus. Adopt an optimistic philosophy and devise a plan that will get you batting 400. Many baseball greats have come from behind. Baseball Hall of Famer Al Kaline, dubbed "Mr. Tiger" had difficulty getting through high school, Mickey Mantle once battled osteomyelitis a potentially crippling disease. We all know how Jackie Robinson persevered a flagrant discriminatory atmosphere to play in the big leagues.

So, the next time you are teetering on the edge, struggling to find the sweet spot to propel you into a grand slam victory, remember the words of Yogi Berra who got it right when he said, "It ain't over, 'till it's over."

# Lesson from a Super Hero

WE ALL LOVE ROLE MODELS with extreme powers. Kids are wild about Iron Man, Spider-Man, or Super Woman. My superhero is an 80 something-year-old woman named Judith. This lady may not be able to "leap tall buildings in a single bound," or have extraordinary powers, but she deserves the super title.

This octogenarian role models kindness, the inner strength of steel, and, most of all, tenacity. A few years ago, Judith completed her first novel. In an era where many authors self publish, my writer friend wanted her work recognized and taken to market by a publisher.

For months she crafted numerous skillful query letters pitching her book and, in return, received polite no thank you rejection emails and messages. When most authors would have turned to self-publishing and released a masterpiece into the world, Judith stood firm, stayed positive, and never gave up.

Does this story about my superhero have a happy ending? You bet. A traditional publishing house issued her book. Judith feels there is no shame in self-publishing and applauds others for the "do it yourself, get it done and on Amazon approach." It just was not her style.

The moral of this story is easily recognizable, right? It's about not settling. It takes a considerable amount of tenacity to stay the course. There is a quote, "The road to success is dotted with many tempting parking places" (author unknown), which describes the vast majority of individuals who get discouraged and stop short of the goal line. Yes, I admit, I sometimes belong to that tribe.

Superheroes like Judith face the challenges head-on and do not quit proving to the rest of us it can be done. I witnessed her fierce determination each time she flexed her courage muscles and flashed a determined grin as she wadded a rejection letter and tossed it into the nearest recycle can.

Are you discouraged and thinking about quitting due to your lack of success in accomplishing a goal? If so, I urge you to reconsider. Find a superhero and study his or her qualities for inspiration. Sure, like the champions, you will encounter some hard knocks on the road to success. Learn to suck it up and keep moving forward. Continue to build your courage and renew your commitment to your goals today.

A final tip from our published author: "PERSEVERE, PERSEVERE, PERSEVERE." She found that powerful sentence on the walls of the home of her writing mentor. It paid off for Judith. It can work for you too.

# Tenacity

In Summary:

* Practice flexibility
* Be a dragon-slayer
* Recount hard-won lessons
* Utilize an objective lens
* Escalate when necessary
* Draw on your willpower
* Don't settle
* Think no matter what
* Invest in your goal
* No slacking off
* No excuses
* Find the sweet spot

# Values
# Your Life Compass

"Good values are like a magnet.
They attract good people"

— JOHN WOODEN

# Monopoly Lessons
# from a Six-Year-Old

I ONCE GAINED A MEMORABLE life lesson while playing Monopoly with my two young nieces. During the game, Alina, who was six, decided she wanted to gift some cash to her sister, whose bank account was rapidly dwindling. When I asked Alina why she would give money away, she simply replied she had more than enough. At that moment, I wondered which lesson to impart. Was it more relevant to explain the game's object was winning, or should I cast the rules aside and let Alina continue with her act of kindness?

I needn't have struggled with the decision because Aisaylnn, her ten-year-old sister, wisely stepped up to field this coaching moment. She very sweetly lavished praise on Alina and made it clear how much she appreciated the gesture. Aisalynn then explained a win was more meaningful if earned fairly.

Without missing a beat, the game continued leaving me with a warm glow over what I had just experienced. The life-lesson lingered with me throughout the day, causing me to examine my actions. How often have I acknowledged I had more than enough? Do I give generously and frequently? Do I possess the bigheartedness of a little girl? Having pondered this, I decided a kindness campaign is something to keep on the front burner.

One of the labels I assign to myself is a tracker. Weighing, measuring, and logging results are motivational in my world. Alina's charitable example prompted me to initiate a Kindness Journal. It is highly motivating to know that daily I must log in a minimum of three benevolent or thoughtful acts to keep me in grace. Sometimes my actions involve giving physical items away as I have more than enough. Other deeds may be as simple as reaching an item from the top shelf in the grocery for someone in a wheelchair.

My challenge for you this week is to take kindness to heart by acting on it daily. Make a caring gesture expecting nothing in return. Typically your kind deed will grow legs. Here's some information about our brain: scientists have coined the term "upstream reciprocity" to explain your act of generosity inspires others to pay it forward. Another bonus: givers experience a brain boost in a release of endorphins, which are "feel-good" chemicals.

Each night when I complete my journal entries, I cannot help but smile and think how much you can learn by playing a board game with a six-year-old.

# Do It Anyway

My friend Esther is an exceptional individual. She is one of those rare "do it anyway" people. Generous beyond measure, she is the first to aid a friend, a foe, or a stranger. Esther's kind deeds have touched the lives of many. She serves as a role model for the community, her children and me, while spending her life paying it forward.

The other day over lunch, I could tell something was bothering my virtuous friend. After a bit of dancing around with the "oh it's nothing" line, she finally looked me in the eye and, with a deep sigh, confessed to feeling saddened by a friend's action. In her typically do-good style, Esther came to an associate's aid by paying her tuition to a self-development class, with no strings attached. While enrolling in the sixteen-week workshop, her friend expressed sincere gratitude. The problem arose at week four when the woman dropped out complaining bitterly about the instructor and the other students. She cited multiple factors to justify walking away from Esther's generous investment in her future.

It is evident to me my charitable friend had no regrets about assisting the woman. Her concern was the missed opportunity. Completing the course would have helped this individual both personally and professionally. I asked my friend if there was a lesson learned for her in this situation. She gave me her warm, loving 1,000-watt smile and said yes, "do it anyway."

If you are familiar with the verses written on the wall of Mother Teresa's home for children, in Calcutta, India, you understand the mantra. The first phrase is: "People are often unreasonable, irrational and self-centered. Love them anyway." People like Esther, who offer kindness with no expectations, have a pure heart and a positive mindset.

The act of unconditional giving is no easy feat. Most of us are looking for a bit of emotional payback, perhaps a smidgeon of recognition, or a minute to bask in the warm glow of expressed gratitude. We often feel cheated when denied a heartfelt thank you. Esther and other individuals with her mindset understand that expecting reciprocity limits the pureness of the gift. Caring, unselfish deeds have inherent emotional benefits. Test this by performing an unconditional kindness this week. By giving with no expectation, you will experience a sense of peace and joy, which is an incentive to "do it anyway."

# Zig or Zag – Your Choice!

I WOKE UP AROUND 3:00 am in a cold sweat. As I gained my bearings and shook off the remnants of a bad dream, the previous day's happenings came flooding back to me. Darn! In a vulnerable moment, I made an extremely unwise decision. I agreed to accept a volunteer leadership position. Sure, I could do the job, but it would take a significant amount of time I did not have. It suddenly occurred to me that it was possible to rescind my acceptance; after all, only 24 hours had passed. Sighing deeply, I knew in my heart that was not an option. Staying true to my word is embedded in my moral code.

Yes, by accepting the appointment, I zigged when I should have zagged. Caught off balance, I did not take the time to think through my priorities. For the entire next year, I sucked-it-up honored my commitment and performed at my best. Admittedly, it was a huge price to pay. Many of my personal goals were put on hold to focus on my role within the organization.

In all honesty, I never regretted the decision to honor my word. In the book *The Four Agreements*, shamanic teacher Don Miguel Ruiz advises to "be impeccable with your word." I believe there is a significant penalty for not doing so. We have all been disappointed by broken promises. When individuals talk a big game but fail to deliver, they lose both respect and credibility. If we discover that pattern in a person, we simply stop listening.

Sadly I've noticed a movement away from firm assurances. Often upon scheduling an event, people offer to call or text to confirm on the day of the engagement. What does that mean? If something better comes up, they may bump you from their schedule? Flexibility is sometimes appropriate, but be aware of the impact staying flexible has on others. Recently two individuals asked me to rearrange someone else's schedule to accommodate their wishes. They probably did not realize the request implied I should prioritize their schedule over giving my word of commitment to the other parties. Gently and respectfully, I declined to do so.

Occasionally life thwarts our ability to keep our word by tripping us up with an emergency. I read once that Oprah, a firm believer in honoring commitments, fell ill and had to cancel an important event, which of course, is understandable.

In controllable situations, always keep your word. And don't bother calling me to confirm, if I said I'd be there, just count me in!

# Loyalty Lessons from a Furry Friend

WHEN I CLOSE MY EYES, I can picture his adorable furry little face. One bright eye surrounded with black fur, the other bordered with fluffy white. He would stand in the upstairs loft, his small head sticking out through the railings looking down and waiting. His name was Ollie, and he had the patience of Job. Daily he would wait hours for my return.

On evenings when I was out of town on business, my husband would try to distract him with treats and games. Ollie stood his ground waiting for me to return until lights out. He wanted to be the first to greet me when I walked through the door. My sweet Shih Tzu companion was the most loyal friend I ever had. Ollie offered up unconditional love.

Loyalty is a precious commodity. Isn't it a characteristic we want most from a friend? When we bare our soul to a trusted cohort, we need to know our vulnerabilities and innermost thoughts are safely locked away like writings in our private journal.

It is important to remember when you bestow the gift of loyalty upon a friend, you take on a noteworthy responsibility. This form of fidelity gets tested when you become privy to a seductive secret confession. Giving your oath to uphold a confidence requires restraint. Breaking that seal of trust destroys credibility and devastates friendships.

Loyalty is a virtue; however, when a friend or lover commits to stick by you, protect you, laugh with you and help dry your tears during a turbulent period, allegiance is a supremely precious gift. A loyalist "has your back," meaning so much more than holding a friend's hand when she is frightened. It means supporting her as she rebuilds her confidence. We sometimes need to check in with ourselves over the loyalty issue. Are we "walking the talk" when we pledge our commitment? Do our actions prove our commitment, or do we use empty words giving the perception of devotion?

Deepak Chopra said it best. The new age guru blogged that "Loyalty balances self-interest. It is the willingness to look out for us and not just me." Our actions speak volumes when we put our loyalty principals into practice.

Lastly, the term means being faithful. When I reflect and remember Ollie, the adorable ten-pound ball of fur, I remain awestruck by his dedication. As I recall all the long hours he spent patiently waiting for me, I cannot think of a better example of loyalty.

# Potatoes Don't Grow
# Behind Your Ears

THE OTHER DAY MY SEVEN-YEAR-OLD niece Aisalynn was getting ready for bed. She finished her bath when her father inquired if she washed behind her ears. She mumbled an affirmative, perhaps not convincingly, so her father posed the question a second time. Aisalynn then distinctively answered yes in a robust assertive voice and inquired why her father repeated the same question twice. Her dad gave a knowing smile, cautioning that potatoes would grow behind her ears if she neglected washing.

Baffled by the statement, my niece challenged him on how he learned about this mysterious spud garden. Her dad replied the lesson came from his grandfather to which Aisalynn countered, "I think your grandfather was joking!" Grandpa's garden theory held no credibility to the wise child of seven. She not only registered disbelief but also announced that Gramps liked making up funny stories.

Whether you're seven or beyond seventy, this incident smacks of the importance of credibility. Wikipedia reports credibility is composed of two key factors – trustworthiness and expertise. Webster says it's the "quality or power of inspiring belief." My simplistic version is this - know your subject well and stay true to your word. Establishing pure truth in our business and personal transactions, in the promises we make to others, and the message we send to the world equates to being honorable and trustworthy.

Building credibility is important, but maintaining it is vital. You can develop this honorable characteristic by committing to total candor. Sounds easy enough, but at times can be a daunting task. For example, say you make a poor decision at work that affects business. Your credibility suffers immediately if you don't own up to it. Honorable individuals swallow their pride; admit the error, and work to find a solution.

The next rule in establishing credibility is, no guessing. Trying to sound like an authority when you are not is deceptive and sends misinformation into the world. As English writer and critic Samuel Johnson stated, "Integrity without knowledge is weak and useless, and knowledge without integrity is dangerous and dreadful."

Keep your word. Never agree to a project, offer to help a friend, or schedule an appointment unless you fully intend to honor your commitment. Conversely, going back on your word is the fastest way to destroy credibility. One misstep in the follow-through department causes customer losses, damaged relationships, and severe disappointment to those who counted on you.

Stay true to your word and check your facts before disseminating information. Protect your reputation, and you'll never run the risk of being called out by a seven-year-old.

# Straight Up

RECENTLY I WAS THE GUEST speaker at an American Business Women's Association meeting. My presentation was entitled "Musings from a Bag Lady." To illustrate the speech, I gave attendees a bag of objects. Each item in the sack represented a life lesson featured in my talk. For example, one object was a straight pin relating to my advice about straight talk, stressing the importance of honesty.

I enjoyed creating the bags and working on my positive strategy musings. Initially, I viewed the project as another speaking presentation; however, the saying is, "you teach what you need to learn." It's funny how that works. As I scripted each item of discussion, I did some soul searching.

The straight pin was top of mind. Did I sometimes tell little white lies? Answer...yes. Is this behavior a method to protect others from bruised egos? Do I sometimes omit the truth to avoid conflict? Answer...yes and yes. Upon reflecting on the lesson I was about to teach, I vowed to be more mindful of "walking my talk" and staying true to honesty values.

Sometimes we would rather withhold our truth to avoid clashing with others and dealing with conflicting viewpoints.

Granted, it is so much easier to vent-off our frustrations to a third party. The problem with that strategy is nothing gets resolved.

How should we deal with sticky situations? Let's say a co-worker steamrolls you at a meeting by using aggressive behavioral tactics. While you are talking, she disagrees, impatiently talks over you, forcing her point and eventually gaining buy-in from the group. You are left silently fuming, considering your options. You can thank her for her input and restate your position. If she was convincing, you might have lost that battle, but you need not suffer further damage to your self-esteem.

The fact is people respect honesty. Resolve a situation like this, by taking action, and speaking your truth. I recommend initiating a 24-hour cooling-off period and then calling her to schedule a meeting over coffee. Be calm, open, and forthright as you explain how her behavior was offensive. My guess is she may seem surprised that she upset you. Perhaps she means it sincerely, or she might be acting. It doesn't matter. You succeeded in delivering the message regarding her unprofessional behavior. Trust me, if you were very clear, she got the signal and verbally or silently respected you for calling her out.

Carry the straight talk framework to all areas of life. You can use the same tactic with you brother-in-law who loves to be a bit of a bully and then claims he was just kidding.

When my speech was over, I taped a straight pin to my vision board to keep this life lesson in front of me. Straight talk is not always easy. But it's a skill worth honing. I speak the truth when I say you can eliminate barriers and misconceptions by being open and transparent.

# The Companion
# of Wisdom

I'VE RECENTLY BECOME INVOLVED IN a massive project, one that will have a significant impact on my life. It's not a solo venture. A partner joins me. This endeavor has many moving parts; I do not always have full control and sometimes may rely on others to reach a successful outcome. Daily I touch all the bases by data diving for pertinent facts, meeting with the players for status updates, and sometimes engaging in lengthy debates with my partner on whether we take a radical step forward or remain in a wait and see a pattern.

Getting to the finish line requires employing all of the above, but the most challenging factor is patience. There are days when I receive progress updates and smile contently knowing on some future date we'll bust out the champagne, raise glasses, and do a victory lap. On other days, I'm so frustrated I want to kick some butt and engage in a bout of heavy-duty ranting. Notice, I said, "want to." Giving way to my baser instincts is not the answer. It would accomplish only the fleeting relief that follows venting.

I am guilty of undervaluing patience and lack the ability to take a pause and wait calmly. You've been there, right? How do we get ourselves to surrender to time instead of demanding it now? Several strategies can be employed to ease frustration and return to the land of peace and harmony.

Let's begin with the glass-half-full viewpoint. Review your progress to date with pride. Embarking on challenging projects takes courage and fortitude, which is cause for at least one high five. Consider the milestones. Moving from phase one to the next level counts for a fist bump or two.

Find inspiration by engaging in a flashback moment. Think of a time when exercising patience brought great rewards. Saint Augustine nailed it when he professed, "Patience is the companion of wisdom." When impatience threatens, suck it up and let your wiser angel take the lead.

Remind yourself that patient people enjoy a healthier mental outlook. We can all make ourselves bat-shit crazy, spiking blood pressure to scary levels.

Change your thoughts. When my partner claimed I was obsessing over the situation, I didn't particularly appreciate hearing it. It turns out he was right. Making the pivot, I focused on other things that restored tranquility and created a more pleasant me.

Few of us have Job's patience, but like any other skill, we rarely get it right the first time. With practice, we can improve. Things worth waiting for take time. In my case, sooner would be better than later, but I'm practicing patience. And that's a good thing.

# Values

In Summary:

* Give unconditionally
* Be faithful and loyal
* Be generous
* Pay it forward
* Maintain your credibility
* Keep your word
* Walk your talk
* Speak your truth
* Value patience

# Negativity Blast Brain Bias

"You'll never find a rainbow if you're looking down."

— CHARLIE CHAPLIN

# The Trouble with Eloise

I HAVE A FRIEND I call "If Only Eloise." Of course, her real name isn't Eloise, and to be honest with you, she is not exactly a friend. My last conversation with Eloise consisted of a litany of laments. It went like this, "If only I had completed my master's degree, if only I stayed with my second husband, if only...well, you get the picture. Not only is "If Only Eloise" focused on the past, she rarely conjures up a positive memory.

As I listened to Eloise drone on, I visualized smashing a rear-view mirror into a zillion little pieces, sweeping it up into a container and burying it deep in the earth. Her self-imposed stress was having an unpleasant effect on me. I wanted to reach out and shake this woman who was intent on wasting precious time by ruminating over the past. When she paused to breathe, I tried a tough-love technique of mine by suggesting she start living in the present.

At times we all fall into an unhealthy "if only" pattern. Meditating on your failures not only adds to your stress level, but it also drains you of energy and diminishes your self-esteem. If you find yourself agonizing over the past, I have some suggestions. First, what could you do to remedy the situation? Do you owe someone an apology? If so, graciously and sincerely ask for forgiveness. If that ship has sailed and you have no recourse, begin by forgiving yourself.

Next, absorb the lesson learned. We all make mistakes; however, the real danger is, making the same mistake twice. So, take a step back, analyze what you could have done differently. Vow to never repeat that action and move on. In the process, cut yourself some slack, treat yourself kindly, and hold yourself in love.

Banish any nasty negative voices in your head by turning your thoughts to positive endeavors. Make an inventory of your strong points. If you must revisit the past, focus on your wins.

When you feel anxiety regarding past mistakes creep in and spill into the moment, stop and center yourself by taking several slow deep breaths. Pull air deep into your diaphragm. Use this breathing technique to slow down your thoughts and rid your mind of harmful intrusions.

Lastly, throw away your rearview mirror. Unless it is attached to your vehicle, it is not a useful tool, only a distraction. Got the picture? Now proceed to dream big, live well, and make the most of each moment.

# Gremlins Be Gone

CLICKING OFF THE PHONE, I glanced at the clock. My client and I spent much of the session dealing with a gang of nasty gremlins in her head. No, she didn't hear strange voices. You can probably relate if I call these nay-saying irritants by the common term of negative self-talk. Sounds familiar now, right? Yes, at times, we all succumb to the power of our built-in saboteurs, allowing them to bombard us with numerous reasons why we cannot accomplish our goals.

Beware, dear reader. Giving an audience to these head demons is a dangerous business. It can damage self-esteem. Our thoughts and actions during waking hours are influenced when we continue listening to the chatter.

So what is the answer to ridding a round-robin of pessimistic thoughts? First, get out of your head. Those gremlins can only bog you down if you allow it. I read there is no off switch to negative self-talk, but I beg to differ. Who's in charge here? You are, of course. Ever walk out of a movie theater because the film was a total waste of time? Apply the same technique. Shift your focus. Redirect your thoughts by flipping on the radio and singing, reading a book, or engaging in a challenging online game.

Inner critics are sneaky and try to go unnoticed. Learn to recognize the gremlin and think about labeling it by name. When Nellie the Nag shows up taunting you with thoughts like, "you can't stick to your diet, you lack will power, just give it up," recognize it as destructive and try talking back. Replace the critical dialogue with positive statements or mantras, and Nellie will get the message she is ousted. It might sound a bit silly, but it is another technique that works.

You can also try writing out a negative statement on paper. (Use paper so you can dramatically destroy it.) After you get a good laugh at how stupid the words look, take it to the nearest shredder or burn it proving the words have no power over you.

The bottom line is, there are many ways to beat the beast. Renowned psychiatrist Carl Jung would advise embracing the negative input. It sounds counterintuitive but acknowledging you are letting the chatter happen may help loosen its clamp on you.

This week develop a keen awareness of any negative thoughts bouncing around in your head. Rid them with a suggested technique. Most importantly, know that you deserve only positive and kind words to describe the real you.

# Prickly People

How do you fare in dreamland? My husband often dreams of flying. I've read people who soar above the clouds in their dreams are confident of achieving their goals. That description fits him well. Last night I was lost in dreamland and found myself wandering into a series of hotels seeking directions from a trio of very testy concierges. This morning it occurred to me that recently I encountered a prickly member of a hotel staff who seemed quite bothered when I asked for help finding a particular conference room. Waiving me off, she told me to try the check-in desk where I eventually received a competent answer.

I remember muttering to myself how ill-suited the individual was for a customer service job. Rude people do not usually get under my skin, but it's apparent somewhere deep in my subconscious the incident smoldered and resurfaced in a dream.

There is no getting around it. We all encounter and deal with difficult people. On my good days, it isn't my practice to go around muttering about a person's behavior. I shrug it off and remind myself not to take it personally. On my best days, I try to respond with kindness. In Don Miguel Ruiz's book *The Four Agreements,* the author developed a premise that "Nothing others do is because of you." My simple request for directions probably had nothing to do with the treatment I received. Perhaps the concierge struggled with a personal problem or under pressure to resolve an urgent situation for another guest.

Yes, living out the "don't take it personally" strategy is challenging, and we don't always have to take it. Dealing with consistent rudeness calls for action. If your co-worker, friend or mother-in-law has a habit of tossing sarcastic barbs your way, it's time for a serious discussion. People sometimes fall into negative behavioral patterns without realizing the effect their delivery has on others. It only takes a few minutes to offer up a gentle reminder that words can hurt. Or, if that doesn't have the desired effect, you might have to stand firm and request the sarcasm comes to an end. If possible, when confronting an offender, try resorting to humor. Nothing diffuses a negative encounter better than a good laugh.

Sometimes it's best to ignore a rude comment. Let it go because stewing over it serves no purpose. That day, after analyzing my dream, I realized I was holding onto pent-up emotions. I quickly sent a silent blessing to the concierge wherever she was and whatever she was doing. With a smile, I moved on to enjoy my day.

Do you have a kind blessing to deliver? If so, don't delay. You never know, it may end up improving someone's disposition. If not, at least you will experience peace.

# Look Down At Your Toes

THOSE WHO KNOW ME UNDERSTAND I'm a happiness addict. Color me passionate about the study of happiness. The fabricated word for me is Eudaimonologist, (or so I'm told) if we use the Greek term eudaimonia for happiness. Whenever I discover a new book about happiness, I consume it and make it part of my collection.

The latest addition to my happiness library is *15 Things You Should Give Up to Be Happy,* by Luminita Saviuc, a Romania blogger, who like me, professes happiness is not just a birthright; it's a skill anyone can cultivate.

Here's where it gets interesting. Unlike me, Luminita experienced a tragic childhood. I'm talking unbelievably dark. When she was ten years old, her extremely abusive father discovered one of his children ate some candy he wanted for himself. Consequently, although she was not even the guilty party, he set Luminita's toes on fire. Pretty amazing that an individual with this beginning in life can advise on creating a life filled with happiness and contentment.

Before she could learn to let light into her world, the author had to let go of her past. Imagine how difficult that was when, for many years, she experienced abuse in a violent environment. Somewhere along her difficult journey, Luminita had an epiphany. She realized taking charge of her life, and moving into the happy zone could only be accomplished when she let go of all that was harmful and toxic. Stop and think about that for a moment.

Any chance you cling to recollections of a time when you felt victimized? Revisiting those painful memories and reliving the hurt will only serve to keep you prisoner to the past, so why continue? As Luminita points out, you must let it go. Okay, I get it. It's not easy to make peace with past hurts, but you can never experience a life transformation until you do, as the author realized.

Need a boost in getting there? If you feel you need help, please consider therapy. If you can go it alone, begin by committing to it. Say it out loud, write it in your journal and tell your best friend that you are no longer dwelling on the past. Make a deliberate choice to free your life of emotional pain. If you find yourself regressing, look down at your toes. No one set them on fire, right? Use them to step into a bright future.

# Be a Believer

LAST WEEK MY HUSBAND AND I attended a variety show at a local theater, an event we look forward to every year. Our town abounds with local talent. In addition to the incredible entertainment, I love watching the interview clips shown before each act. One segment revealed a young man in his early 30's who announced he finally started believing in himself enough to audition. I heartily applauded that positive statement. Putting yourself out there takes a significant dose of self-confidence.

A large sign in my office states: Believe. I've hung it on the wall to remind both my clients and me to stop doubting ourselves. Too often, we give in to self-sabotage. Our 30-something entertainer used a simple technique that is very powerful in developing and maintaining self-esteem. Want to know the secret to his success? He stopped listening to his nagging inner critic. We all have one, you know. I've given mine a name: Stormy.

From time to time, my gremlin swoops in over-stocked with gloom and doom, always predicting failure. I've learned to recognize the negative voice in my head and send that bully packing. Like Stormy, all inner gremlins are fear-based. They thrive on status quo, wanting nothing to do with progress and change.

Successful people possess a commonality regarding self-belief. They've learned to ignore the critics in their heads and staunchly refuse to let an ounce of doubt enter the picture. Children don't deal with negative thoughts. They believe they can do anything. When my niece Alina was six, she was the poster child for believing in her capabilities. The giant-sized moxie in her pint-sized package was most impressive. I'm confident when Alina's gremlin came calling; she burst into fits of giggles thinking, don't be silly; of course I can do that.

Whether you're six, seventy-six, or beyond, if you are auditioning for a Broadway musical or interviewing for a job as a design engineer, the key to accomplishing your dreams is confidence. Internal and external critics cannot drag you down without your consent. You are in control. When your gremlin tries to dissuade you from accomplishing your dreams, remember the sage advice from one of the masters, Vincent Van Gogh, "If you hear a voice within you say you can't paint, then by all means paint, and that voice will be silenced."

Are you getting ready to put yourself out there and strut your stuff? I applaud you. Begin by flexing your self-esteem muscle. Then wear your confidence like armor and rock it!

# Newsflash: Accentuate the Positive

As I plunked down my groceries during an early morning food run, the clerk apparently full of caffeine, and a daily news dose began his tirade. He proceeded to bombard me with a laundry list of negative world happenings as my grocery items were scanned and tallied. I scrutinized his troubled face as I mentally cringed from the blows of his pessimistic newsflash.

When the grocer stopped to take a breath, I suggested he stop taking in all the negative news. He looked at me as if my brain were as blond as my hair and crisply informed me bad news was the only kind available. I proposed he create some good news. Offering up some sincere gratitude for his service and my brightest smile, I left him to ponder what I meant.

Admittedly my neighborhood grocer wasn't, all wrong, when he informed me of the bad news ratio. According to Psychology Today, media studies show negative news far outweighs good news. For every 17 adverse news reports, we hear only one, positive news report. Taking in all this negativity drives us to fear. When that happens, our stress hormone, cortisol, kicks in. When overextended, we can drown in that hormone, causing harm to our bodies. Focus on this fact: cortisol deactivates your body's natural self-repair mechanisms and raises your blood sugar.

As a society, we need to stop obsessing over negative news and start finding a reason to smile. My morning interlude could have been brighter if the clerk shared a positive quote or flashed a winning grin and told me a joke. Humor is contagious. I could have left the store on a high note and paid it forward by telling my next client the joke.

In 1975 Paul Simon had a smash hit song entitled, "50 Ways to Leave Your Lover." Think about it. There must be at least 50 positive ways to kick-start your day, leaving behind the morning habit of filling up on downbeat information. For example, we can get up ten minutes early to pray, meditate, read a funny story, write in a gratitude journal, repeat positive affirmations, or listen to an uplifting podcast. Buddha reminds us "Every morning we are born again." Remember that tomorrow morning. If you must flip on CNN before your feet hit the floor, train your brain to remain positive.

# View From 30,000 Feet

EVER WATCH TWO KIDS GET in a tussle and be given a time out? I witnessed this occurrence recently. Sentenced to separate spaces, two little boys tearfully dragged their tiny feet to the appointed corner to wait out the clock. What happened next can only be attributed to the blissful innocence of childhood. Thirty seconds into the time-out Little Boy A became entranced in the scurrying of a rather large ant as the insect traversed the wall. Meanwhile, Little Boy B found his neon green shoelace a suitable object to remove from his shoe and twirl around his fingers. What was supposed to be a quiet time of reflection and repentance was quickly converted into exploring other options.

When the bell went off, signaling punishment was over, a supervising adult told both boys to apologize and shake hands. They did so grinning and giggling, probably not even remembering or caring about the earlier disagreement. It never occurred to them to hold a grudge or debate who was in the wrong.

Children have the innate ability to move on quickly. No muss, no fuss, no hard feelings. They simply resume fun and frolic. Not always the case with adults. We sometimes dwell on frustrating situations long past the event. Ever catch yourself replaying an incident over and over in your head like a bad dream? Or do you complain about the injustice to anyone who will listen? How about the inability to quickly rebound from making a mistake, losing a sale, or missing an urgent deadline? Do you find yourself ruminating over those events?

Whether it's mentally beating yourself up for a blunder, or clinging tightly to the memory of an unfair situation, it's time wasted! You can get from stomach-in-knots anxiety to peaceful calm in two steps.

First, reframe the situation by examining it objectively from 30,000 feet. If you lost the big sale, list the reasons your customer said no. Perhaps there were things you could have done differently. Make a note of those actions and consider it a lesson learned. Next, remind yourself the past cannot be changed. It's over, time to move on.

Are you still feeling a high level of anxiety? I recommend invoking the 24-hour rule. If you must ruminate on a situation, time it out. Then, like the little tykes, when the bell rings signaling you've spent an entire day and night fretting and employing negative self-talk, stop the nonsense and come out smiling. Let your negative thoughts evaporate into the dawn of a new day. Focus on the positive and do something that makes your heart sing.

# Negativity

In Summary:

- Stop self-sabotage
- Banish internal critics
- Adopt a positive mantra
- Learn to let go
- Find a reason to smile
- Share a great joke
- Pray
- Journal
- Don't take it personally
- Bless others
- Toss your rear-view mirror
- Forgive

# Relationships
# Connecting With Heart

"For beautiful eyes, look for the good in
others, for beautiful lips, speak only words
of kindness; and for poise, walk with the
knowledge that you are never alone."

— AUDREY HEPBURN

# Finding Comfort in an Uphill Battle

As I sat at my desk attending a virtual conference call, the CEO, Keith, shared a story about his weekend bike trip. Listening to him recount the outing, I knew we had nothing in common when it came to biking. My ideal ride was around the block on my beach cruiser. Keith's joy ride was an uphill climb ascending eight miles to an elevation of 5,000 feet. Whoa! Indeed not my idea of fun. I mentally categorized this type of biking event as one of those extreme sports requiring a high level of physical exertion and a ton of guts. Count me out.

As the story unfolded, our hero came to a point in the ride when he felt totally spent. Pushing uphill for miles drove him to exhaustion. Based on his training, he engaged in some mental exercises to steady his nerves and renew his spirit. Failing miserably at his attempt, Keith was ready to give up. Within seconds his friend, an athlete with superior biking skills, rode alongside him and gently put his hand on Keith's back. As they continued the climb, the two were compatibly silent, revealing the supportive touch was just the magic the executive needed to complete the trek to the summit.

Keith did have to explain why he told the story. It wasn't to prove he is a goal-oriented guy who enjoys a significant challenge. We already knew that. The narrative illustrated how a little teamwork, or a touch of inspiration at the right time, could make a huge difference. The anecdote lingered with me all week, like the remnants of a vivid dream. I decided to mindfully monitor my actions to make sure I do my part to assist others on their uphill journey.

Whether it takes place in a corporation, a family relationship, or an interaction between strangers, the literal or symbolic outstretched hand brings immeasurable benefits to both the giver and the receiver. No doubt, the guy who had Keith's back experienced a mood boost as he watched his buddy continue up the trail. The feel-good frame of mind continued as Keith paid it forward by reliving the experience for us. Although the meeting was virtual, I felt connected and enveloped in a warm glow extending out into the various locations of 65 coaches. As the call came to a close, I knew we all were looking for the next opportunity to lend a hand.

# A Message The Heart Understands

I LEANED IN, OFFERING MY friend the comfort of a warm hug telling her I'd see her soon. We'd spent an hour together over coffee. She was going through a rough patch and needed a listening ear. Let's face it; there is no better remedy to help heal the hurts than attentive compassion coupled with an embrace.

As I walked to my car, I thought about the power of a hug. Did you know that studies conducted on the human touch revealed that both the "toucher" and the "touchee" experience actual physiological benefits from human contact? According to researcher Dr. Dolores Krieger, in techie talk, it goes like this: red blood cells carry hemoglobin, a substance transporting oxygen to the body tissue. When one person lays hands on the other, the hemoglobin levels in both parties' bloodstream increases, which can aid healing. Hugging also causes our muscles to relax, which can help ease the stress we experience during the day.

Want to develop a healthier relationship? Hug more! There is a scientific reason why active hugging leads to bonding. It produces that awesome feel-good hormone oxytocin, also dubbed as the cuddle chemical. As in the embrace exchanged between my friend and myself, a hug also increases empathy and understanding. When words fail, hugging telegraphs a message the heart understands.

Hit by a bout of the blues? Enfold yourself in a firm hug from a loved one, or initiate a little one-on-one cuddle time with your pet. More scientific data: Hugging increases serotonin production from your brain, which can elevate both your mood and your self-esteem.

Hugs are beneficial for individuals of all ages, but studies show hugging becomes even more critical as we age. Hugging decreases stress hormones that inhibit the immune system, so get in the habit of doling out daily hugs.

One final pointer, when you go in for a hug, do it right like my friend Jay. Make it a hearty embrace. A hug must last for at least 20 seconds to be beneficial.

High fives are great, but hugs are healing. They build confidence and spread joy. By strengthening bonds and showing understanding, we open our hearts to others. So hug your kid, hug your dog and hug a senior. If you're feeling brave, hug a stranger. And next time we meet, forget the handshake, let's embrace!

# The Perfect Breakfast Cookie

I HUNG UP THE PHONE, wondering what I was going to do with all those Girl Scout Cookies. The early morning call boldly interrupted my sleep. My seven-year-old niece, Alina, who lives in Michigan, had no concept of time zones. She launched into how Cranberry Citrus Crisps will be my new favorite cookie of all time with barely a hello. Then she triumphantly crowed this new addition to the Girl Scout cookie program has 9 grams of whole grain and ended by asserting that I should purchase a dozen boxes. Rubbing the sleep from my eyes, I reminded my niece that she was not a Girl Scout or even a Brownie for that matter. I also informed her I had omitted sugar from my diet.

Ignoring my push-back, Alina began spinning a web of charm around me so tightly I could find no wiggle room. Before we terminated the conversation, I consented to buy a half-dozen of the cranberry cookies and three boxes of Rah-Rah Raisins, which Alina claimed made a perfect breakfast because they contained oatmeal and yogurt. As we hung up, she told me how much she loved me and promptly reminded me to add money to cover the shipping charges.

How did a seven-year-old sell me something I did not need or even want for that matter? I'll tell you how. Alina helped her best friend Kerilyn with sales because Keri, as she called her, "Has no sweet aunties to buy her cookies," and concluded by reminding me that I taught her "A friend in need is a friend indeed." Don't you hate it when your words come back to haunt you?

Yes, the friend in need thing got me. I had to support this seven-year-old sales superstar in her effort to be a friend who had Keri's back. If there was one characteristic I wanted my niece to develop throughout her formative years, it was forging strong relationships and being a blessing to others.

Alina's actions always have a profound effect on me. She has a way of making me want to be a better "sweet auntie." I decided I needed to check in on myself to make sure I am "a friend indeed," something we should all keep in mind. And by the way, if you're in the neighborhood, feel free to stop in for coffee and some Cranberry Citrus Crisps. I guarantee they will become your new favorite cookie of all time.

# Counting Connections

A DYNAMIC COMEDY WRITER FACILITATED the workshop I attended. During the class, she asked us to sit with people we didn't know. Our instructions involved a three-minute exercise. She chartered each group to compile a list of things we all had in common. By the time the ending bell sounded, my little band of newfound friends was busy building a rapport. The group began with a fundamental commonality. None of us were native Californians. We branched out into marital status, as we all had spouses and eventually found we shared a love of Italian food. At the end of the three minutes, a budding camaraderie evolved.

The purpose of the warm-up was to connect with others. Whether you are at a cocktail party, in an interview or attending a networking event, building a relationship begins by making a connection. Appropriately utilized, social media is also a viable place to connect with groups of people.

Your network's size and strength reflect the amount of effort you put into making an actual connection that leads to a stable relationship. We all gravitate toward genuine individuals who take an interest in others by asking questions, giving undivided attention, and engaging us with warm smiles and welcoming handshakes. On the flip side of the coin, we all have encountered friends and acquaintances who covet all the airtime during a meeting or use their Facebook posts to let you know it's all about them.

Want to grow your connections into meaningful associations? Begin by merely acknowledging others beyond the perfunctory hellos and lackluster, how are you doing questions. Listen with interest and stay in the moment by offering the other party your total focus. Relinquish your agenda. Make every effort to learn. Connect for the pure joy of getting to know someone.

Bring value to conversations by giving sincere compliments. Be sure to lavish encouragement on those who need an extra boost by offering up a kind word or displaying supportive action. Acknowledge any special events or milestones achieved by those in your network.

Want to know how you're doing? Make a conscious effort to measure your connection activity this week. Tally up how many times you just went through the motions versus the amount of time you spent building relationships. Permit yourself to be the kindest person you know. Generate warmth and generosity. I promise it will be your best week ever!

# Extra Milers Club

AS TREASURER OF A NON-PROFIT organization, I've been collecting donations for our scholarship fund. Each day when the postal carrier arrives, I find pledges from members mixed in with my bills and junk mail. Today as I slit an envelope I found a bonus. My friend, Melody, not only enclosed a generous contribution, she filled the pocket with a cute note, a funny cocktail napkin, and lots of love.

It figures. Melody possesses an attitude of generosity, beginning with her killer smile. She is one of those people who graces her actions with that extra special touch. No doubt, her daily mission is to add unexpected joyful moments to those she encounters. My friend works her magic, making the ordinary extraordinary.

We all have different types of people in our lives. When contrasting the Melodys, who go the extra mile, to others doing just enough to get by, is there any doubt who we should emulate? If you want to be a member of the "extra-milers" club, you can. It just takes a bit of creativity and an extra dose of care.

Begin by observing role models like Melody. Consider how those who champion the art of exceeding the norm sprinkle an extra dose of joy into your life. Got the picture? It's okay to start small. For example, if you're flipping through a social media feed, forego tapping the mechanical "like" button and lavish a sincere compliment on a friend's post.

Think about the stops you make during your day. While picking your son up at school, why not drop off a Starbucks card and sincere note of thanks to the teacher helping him master geometry. Are you en-route to the doctor's office? Entertain the staff with your five best jokes. After dealing with sick people all day, they need a laugh. The same goes for the dentist's office.

Sometimes we neglect gifting those closest to us with out-of-the-box kind deeds. Surprise your spouse with an unsolicited back massage, take your mom to a chick-flick movie or play catch with your dog until he gets exhausted and wants to quit.

Challenge yourself to become a Melody. See how many times you can extend an action beyond the ordinary and make others feel significant and loved. Let's turn that famous quote, "There are no traffic jams on the extra mile," on its ear. Ready? I'll meet you there.

# Friends For Life

THE DAY I MET ERICA, I knew I wanted to be exactly like her. Approximately twenty years later, I'm still aspiring to emulate my friend's many loving characteristics she shares with the world. Although I will probably never reach the level of an Erica clone, I feel humbled by her friendship's immense blessing.

Everyone needs someone like her in their life. She is the type of person who never gives up on me. When discouragement drags me down, Erica lifts me up with sincere words like, "I am confident you will work through it." So I take another swing at whatever it is I'm trying to accomplish because, trust me, when you have that kind of an encourager on your side, you don't want to let her down.

John Donne was right when he wrote, "No Man is an island." Connecting with other human beings is essential to living a happy, balanced life. By cultivating a close circle of friends, you gain numerous perks. Someone like Erica inspires me to reach my goals.

I connect with my friends Irma and Joan when I need a reality check and Shawndra when I need younger woman's perspective. Jeanette, who entered my life when we were toddlers, is the person I connect with to draw strength from my roots. When I'm in danger of veering off-course, friends like Carolyn and Ellen keep me grounded.

There are compelling reasons why friendships are vital to our well-being. According to scientific studies, people who develop strong social relationships are less likely to die prematurely compared to individuals who live isolated. Friends are stress busters. Researchers at UCLA find women often reach out to a BFF while working through upsetting issues. Connecting with someone you share a close bond with can help reduce the stress hormone cortisol.

How flat and dull the good times would be without friends who rejoice in our triumphs. When you ace that primo interview, announce your engagement, or become a parent, celebrating with people who care makes the occasion so much sweeter.

Bottom line - friendships are a two-way street. Long ago you were taught to have a friend you must first learn to be a friend. In keeping a Carolyn, Irma, or Jeanette in our lives, we must give as good as we get. National Friendship Week is supposedly sometime in August, but who cares? Let's celebrate it this week by letting our peeps know how much we value them. I write in gratitude for all the friends (too numerous to name) who have enriched my life. Hats off to friendship!

# Finding Your Tribe

THIS MORNING FINDS ME ON my annual epic purging and organizing mission. In my quest to clear up clutter crowding my closets, I came across a little brown book containing sincere heartfelt writings of The Sisterhood of Traveling Hearts. Who are these sisters? A diverse group of friends who developed a deep bond during early morning hikes in Southern California's Coachella Valley. We gave ourselves the name and the assignment of penning what our relationship meant to us on an individual level in the brown leather book.

Regarding my personal contribution, I did not write about how immensely difficult it was to keep up with these strong, vibrant women. (Yeah, leave it to me as a hiking novice to join a group of serious athletes.) I still have the book Cathy gave each of us, deeming it required reading, *Younger Next Year for Women: Live Strong, Fit and Sexy Until You're 80 and Beyond.* I smile, remembering exhaustion so complete from hiking I could barely turn the pages.

In our written words, there is a common theme. Most pages contained the phrase "life-changing," and reference the fact we each hold a special place in our hearts for our fellow sisters.

Well, advance the clock eight years plus. Since our hiking days, life events occurred, I moved to Florida, and the group no longer hikes together or has many get-togethers, but I can assure you the deep bond remains. And even if it didn't, the time spent together sharing our triumphs and sorrows was indeed life-changing.

Yes, I'm taking a long time getting to the life lesson of this article, but you might have guessed that it's about the importance of forming friendships. It's no secret that friends increase your sense of purpose. According to experts at the Mayo Clinic, friends play a significant role in your overall well-being. (Especially the Cathy's of the world who care so much about your health.)

Developing and maintaining friendships takes focus. If you're new to an area, it takes some effort to find your tribe. You know, those people who care about and really "get you."

So, if you're looking for a group to gather with, whether it is over coffee, book clubs or fitness events, be present. Reach out and join www.meetup.com groups, attend community events, and volunteer. Indulge in new interests, like art, drama, and Tai Chi classes. Join a church or synagogue. If you make yourself available to open up and share your life, you will find your tribe.

# Revisiting
# Networking 101

LIKE MOST ENTREPRENEURS, I AM always happy to pass on a referral. Many small business owners gain a portion of their business by word of mouth. Recently I referred a friend to a service provider. I did not know the person I was recommending, but felt confident as one of my trusted networking contacts gave me the green light. As a heads-up and to introduce myself, I gave the individual a call. She thanked me for the referral, dismissing it as a fait accompli.

I hung up somewhat perplexed. Networking and referrals are not one-directional. I presented the woman with an opportunity to bid on a job, but had she put forth more effort, she could have gained so much more.

In her book, *Nonstop Networking: How to Improve Your Life, Luck, and Career,* Andrea R. Nierenberg explains, "Networking is the process of developing and maintaining quality relationships that are mutually beneficial." Simply put, networking is about building connections, not about scoring a lead. My interaction with the vendor might have ended on a different note if rather than resting on her laurels; she spent a few moments telling me about her services. Why not invite me to check out her website and read testimonials written by people who benefited from hiring her. Then to secure our connection, she could have switched gears and inquired about my business.

Any student of Networking 101 knows creating connections and nurturing relationships ends up benefiting both parties over time. Whether you receive a business referral, or a viable lead for your job search, thinking of the activity as a slam-dunk situation is a big mistake. These transactions are more akin to a dance involving partners. Stated differently, think: moving in concert. Then think reciprocity and invest time in others.

In the course of accepting a referral, initiate two actions. One, sincerely thank the person for their time and the lead. Tell them you will sync-up after you have made contact to let them know of the outcome. Next, follow up by asking if there is anything you can do to assist your benefactor.

Take it one step further by putting a thank you in writing. People enjoy receiving appreciation, both audibly and visually. Crafting a short email takes only a moment. Be sincere and caring in all your networking opportunities, and your business and personal relationships will grow. You can bank on it!

# Relationships

In Summary:

* Dispense warm hugs
* Be genuine
* Listen with interest
* Perform out-of-the-box kindness
* Lend a hand
* Find your tribe
* Share your life
* Value your friendships
* Practice gratitude
* Forge strong relationships

# Mindfulness
# It's All Mental

"When we get too caught up in the
busyness of the world, we lose connection
with one another – and ourselves."

— JACK KORNFIELD

# Popsicles and Pockets of Joy

WHEN SHE ARRIVED FOR OUR breakfast date, Dominique's opening statement was, "Every day is a Monday." Responding to my
quizzical expression, she filled in the blanks. Dom, a successful
entrepreneur, is in the process of growing her second business.
This venture means hitting it hard in back-to-back seven-day
work weeks. Understanding the amount of work that goes into a
new business enterprise, I tipped my head in an empathetic nod.

My friend continued talking about her busy life and related
how, while listening to a podcast, she discovered a way to keep
the pace without spiking her stress level. Adhering to a female
combat soldier's advice, Dom cultivated a way to look for and
take advantage of pockets of downtime. For example, when she
has the rare 2-hour chunk of time, she heads home to soak in
her Jacuzzi. An extra thirty minutes is spent in the grocery store
with her headphones on. Dom finds strolling the aisles while list-
ing to soft jazz relaxing as she leisurely accomplishes restocking
her pantry. For a mere 15 minutes, she can find a quiet corner
to sit still and "just be." If her pets are around, Dom indulges

in doggy cuddle time, (stroking a dog is touted by experts as a healthy form of stress relief.)

Author and speaker, Amanda Enayati, is in complete agreement with Dom about mastering "the pause" during a demanding day. In a recent interview, Amanda referred to these portions of downtime as "pockets of joy." Enayati, who authored the book, *Seeking Serenity: The Ten New Rules for Health and Happiness in the Age of Anxiety,* discusses a pause to deal with negative stress. The author recommends not over-thinking the break. Just find a quiet space to rest and renew, or try heading outdoors to commune with nature.

Establishing one of these new rules in your life might take a bit of practice. Like Dom, you must develop an awareness and capture those precious moments of "me" time. By setting up these buffers, you can minimize and neutralize your stress level. A word of caution here: Don't squander it thinking you should use the time to knock off a few more things on your "to-do" list.

Try it with me. This week I'm committing to my pockets of joy by instituting the 80/20 rule. For 20 minutes each day, I'll close my office door, think of nothing, and enjoy my 80 calories cold-brew coffee pop. Bye, bye, toxic stress.

# New Age Productivity

THE OTHER NIGHT MY HUSBAND fell asleep while watching TV. After gently prying the remote out of his hand, I decided to do some channel surfing. Before long, I landed on a sitcom where a wild-eyed blond woman stood with a hairdryer in one hand, maneuvering her electric toothbrush with the other while attempting to shove one leg into her skinny jeans. While the TV audience howled, I stood frozen, unable to utter a single giggle. Why? Well, it wasn't too long ago I caught myself unsuccessfully attempting to accomplish three things at once. The problem is, I know better. I teach time management and ask my clients to commit to "mono-tasking." (Yes, that is a thing).

Research supports the theory that multitasking can be harmful to your health. Do not be fooled! Multitasking is not a time saver because realistically, there is no such thing as attacking two or more tasks simultaneously. The only true multitasking occurs when one act is auto-pilot passive. For example, it is possible to listen to reggae music while whipping up a soufflé.

Conversely, what happens when you are typing an email while chatting on the phone with a friend is a rapid shift between two tasks. In his book, *The Myth of Multitasking*, author and business coach David Crenshaw explains a concept called "switch-tasking," which is toggling back and forth between two tasks.

There are consequences to what we think of as multitasking. If you focus on my article and not merely scan it as you maneuver the line at Starbucks and order a latte, accept this cold, hard truth. When you attempt to perform more than one task simultaneously, your error rate increases along with your stress level, if you completed a singular job, time would be saved rather than squandered.

Mono-tasking is the "new age" productivity. According to Urban Dictionary, "The performance by an individual of one task, and only one task, at a point in time is called mono-tasking." UD further states, "It can be more productive than multitasking as it allows an individual to put all their attention and focus on the task at hand."

Amen. Let's all practice mono-tasking. And that sitcom I was watching had me convulsing in a fit of giggles. The blond protagonist lost her balance halfway into her skinny jeans, tumbled, making a soft landing onto her bed as her hairdryer went flying. The electric toothbrush became entangled in her flaxen curls. I silently thanked her for proving my point.

# The Gift of Presence

AT A RECENT HOLIDAY PARTY, I encountered a young woman at the buffet. As we progressed down the food line, she quickly introduced herself then immediately launched into a monologue. Cindy, my new acquaintance, described herself as, "beyond stressed," about her mega-to-do list. My first reaction was to nod signaling I understood the chaos she was describing but a voice in my head announced that I should suggest she leave the party and attend to more critical tasks before she hit the wall. My verbose inner dialogue had a point; Cindy was not enjoying the moment, nor my company, for that matter.

Following me to a quiet corner, she continued to deliver a laundry list of incompletes between quick bites of food. I doubted her taste buds had time to savor the scrumptious food our hostess prepared. If I knew this young lady better, I would have taken the plate from her hand and led her in some deep breathing exercises to relax. Perhaps next, I'd suggest she either relax and enjoy the party or politely say her good-byes and move on to tackle some of the essential errands needing attention within the next 24 hours.

If you are not mindful in the present moment, then mentally, you are somewhere in your head. What is the point of attending an optional function when you're not engaged and happily enjoying the beauty and warmth of a gathering? Young Cindy is a classic case of someone, overbooked and overburdened. Perhaps if she took a moment to slow down and examine her priorities, Cindy might conclude she was overly ambitious in her plans to be all things to all people. And maybe she would cease loading up her calendar with multiple events and start living mindfully. Numerous benefits exist when we are living in the moment. Mindfulness improves general health issues. Studies on cancer patients prove such techniques enhance the ability to deal with serious illnesses.

There are more perks to paying attention, and one of them is improved personal relations. So, just a reminder to all the Cindy's out there. One of the most precious gifts you can lavish on a stranger, friend, or loved one is your attention. Stop listening with half an ear and make your time together rich with awareness. If you only have fifteen minutes before you dash off to the next event on your list, speak less, and listen more to make those 900 seconds count. If you do, you will leave behind the perfect gift, your presence.

# Making Memories

ARE YOU FAMILIAR WITH THE term: ministry of presence? Until last week, I had never heard the phrase. It was described by one of my favorite bloggers as "An act that blesses people in pain, merely with a presence--by showing up, and offering tangible support, whether it's in the form of a hug, a listening ear or a steaming bowl of soup." Performing an act of kindness is admirable, and we can all do more of that. But for today, let's focus on a simplistic form of this ministry. Just. Be. Present.

You see, I am preparing to spend a week vacationing with family, so I've been reflecting on this Brendan Behan quote: "No yesterdays are ever wasted by those who give themselves to today." That means mindfully paying attention to others. Being in the moment means full-on engagement blocking all other distractions. I've made some promises to myself. Taking the "being present" part seriously, I'm going unplugged. I promise not to use my phone for anything other than capturing memories. No tweeting, texting, or reading emails. I solemnly swear to stay in the moment and make the family my only priority. I'll permit myself to venture off for some sweet solitude, but I'll show up and nurture the relationship in their presence.

It is all too easy to fill our lives with distractions. Tuning out the constant static competing for our mindshare and vying to capture our thoughts is an uphill battle. Penalties should exist for wasting precious moments. When my thoughts stray from soaking up the blissful scenery to wondering how things are going at work, I've instituted a mental dollar in the swear jar type philosophy.

How are you doing on that score? Do you have meaningful dinner conversations, or are you dining with one eye on the big screen and the other on your plate? Have you banned cell phones and texting at the table and made mealtime a period of sharing? Are there some segments of your daily life where you are only half-present and semi-engaged?

Okay, I hear you. Engagement works both ways. I have a tip for you when your spouse is only half-listening. If I try to talk to my husband while the TV is on, he is fake listening, so I use a trick. I politely ask him to please mute, then I stand in front of the television, so he has no choice but to listen up and grant me the ministry of presence. (Don't judge me, it works, but please if you're married to a Canadian, don't try this during hockey season).

This week, practice tuning into others. Give yourself to today and reap the benefits of stronger relationships and sweeter memories.

# Auto-Piloting Danger

LOOKING DOWN AT MY HALF-EMPTY dinner plate, I hardly remembered tasting my food. Puzzled, I began breaking down the past few days that I had labeled as my "klutzy week." Upon reflection, I realized I wasn't just prone to spilling and dropping things, I was operating on auto-pilot, and my pilot was barely awake at the controls.

More often than not lately, my body was in the here and now, but my mind wandered, taking me wherever it wanted to go. Feeling a little mentally mushy, I reminded myself there was no need for panic. Autopilot is beneficial at times. Our brains guide us through established tasks while our thoughts work on problem solving. So, it's okay to let autopilot take control sometimes, but I reprimanded myself for allowing my automated mode far too much power.

The opposite of auto-piloting is mindfulness. My half-eaten meal was a wake-up call. I needed to evoke some strategies to practice awareness. Henrik, a Swedish blogger I follow, recommended three such techniques. The first, hardly a profound suggestion, but none-the-less good advice: slow down. Color me guilty for barreling through mundane tasks causing spills and dropping objects while my mind was somewhere in a far off land.

It stands to reason when we slow the pace; efficiency takes over. Reflecting on this quote helped me ease up and focus: "The feeling that any task is a nuisance will soon disappear if it is done in mindfulness. " - Thich Nhat Hahn.

The second strategy I grasped immediately: Tell yourself – "now I am". Reminding yourself of what you are doing in the present moment does more than prevent your mind from wandering. By remaining aware, we capture and fully appreciate the experience, whether it's observing a hummingbird drink from a flower, watching a child skipping rope, or sipping tangy lemonade.

Ever find yourself ruminating over an issue or beating yourself up for making a mistake? Sure, we are all guilty of that. Reach for the third technique when that occurs by disrupting your inner critic. Speak to that mind-control freak declaring to the little head voice you are not going down that path for the 17th time. Then bring your thoughts back to the present. Let me add one of my go-to's for creating a mindful presence. Change up your routines. Take a new route home, or have breakfast for dinner. If you always read fiction, try absorbing a memoir.

Why not take the mindfulness challenge with me. Stay in the moment by using these simple strategies. It's all mental. Let's do this.

# Mindfulness

In Summary:

* Slow down
* Remain aware
* Change your routine
* Be present
* Unplug
* Tune into others
* Practice mono-tasking
* Seek serenity
* Create "me" time
* Listen more

# Optimism
# Embrace the Sunny Side

"Keep your face to the sunshine and
you cannot see a shadow"

— HELEN KELLER

# The Duck Who Scored

NOTHING DELIGHTS ME MORE THAN a positive thinker. I encountered such an optimist the other day; only this character had feathers. During a walk around the lake, I stopped to observe a Mallard duck studying a swan feeder. It was apparent he wanted dinner, but without the elongated neck of a swan, those food pellets were impossible to reach. I watched sensing that little guy was determined to solve the dilemma. Several minutes later, he astonished me by performing a Michael Jordan jump. The duck went from ground zero to three feet straight up but still could not score a meal.

Who knew ducks could jump? They aren't built for jumping, but my determined feathered friend somehow pushed himself up. This character won my heart. I stepped up to the feeder and grabbed a handful of pellets for my new friend. He quacked. I laughed, and we happily parted ways.

As I continued my walk, I realized the duck reinforced a critical life lesson. There is power in a positive mindset. His optimistic thinking did not solve his dilemma, but it made a significant impression on me, one worth addressing. Positive people are memorable. Win or lose; it makes no difference. These role models inspire and impact others.

Think being optimistic is a bunch of rose-colored-glasses hooey? Not so. According to the psychologist, Michael F. Scheier, optimists are not Pollyannas; they are problem solvers, always working on improving the situation. It was apparent my Mallard friend stepped up his game to solve his problem.

Perhaps you don't feel naturally optimistic and label yourself as a realist. No worries. According to Dr. Srikumar Rao, author of the book, *Are You Ready to Succeed?: Unconventional Strategies for Achieving Personal Mastery in Business and in Life,* we all have the power to rewire our brain. In his Ted Talk, Dr. Rao provides strategies to help plug into our hard-wired happiness and coax out our inner optimist.

Want to work on being more positive? Try conditioning yourself. Create and linger in random moments of positivity while pushing negative thoughts to the background. Too often, we let good moments pass without a second thought. This week, when you experience something pleasant, perhaps as small as spotting the first crocus of spring or sharing a laugh with a friend, savor it.

Consider a problem you've been struggling with, then, think of the duck. If a duck can brainstorm a possible solution, you can too. And if you think about it, his positive thinking worked. Had he not jumped I would never have tossed him the reward.

# Changing Your Stripes

EVER TRY CHANGING YOUR SISTER into a zebra? I came across a video depicting a creative child, perhaps about four years old, who artfully inked zebra stripes on her little sister's body. Why? Well, as she explained to her mother, she loves zebras. Her mother softly admonished her, saying that turning the little tyke into an animal was silly. Quite frankly, I don't think our little artist was buying it.

There is a good deal of logic in the child's thinking. If you love zebras, why not hang out with them? It makes sense to me. And by the way, the toddler turned zebra seemed to be enjoying her new persona.

In a child's world, all things are possible if you use your imagination. I recall visiting my three-year-old niece on one of Michigan's blustery cold days. Amid a beach blanket in the cozy living room sat Aisalynn wearing a bathing suit adorned with a bright coral starfish. The little darling was busy building an imaginary sandcastle. As I waved hello, she smiled and told me she felt like a day at the beach.

In my career coaching practice, I sometimes meet clients who have temporarily misplaced their imagination. Although bored with their jobs, these individuals cannot fathom making a career reinvention. When I bring up the possibility, I often encounter at least 27 reasons why they cannot make a move from a job that makes them dread Monday mornings and long for Friday evening happy hours.

Of all the 27 reasons, the most common refrain stems from fear and confusion. At first blush, they have no idea how the reinvention would end up. What would they do? Well, if we fast-forward our zebra loving little friend by twenty years, she will probably be a veterinarian or end up working in a zoo as an animal trainer. Often it helps to think back and remember cast aside childhood dreams. Perhaps a frustrated female engineer wanted to be a gourmet chef but got sidetracked by parental pressure.

When you stay open to possibilities, it becomes clear that most things are possible. Just fend off fear and anxiety. Add a dose of childlike imagination, optimism, and the belief that your cast aside dream can resurface if you work hard enough.

So, how about it? Are you a zebra lover ready to make a change in your career or personal life? If the answer is yes, I applaud you!

Be forewarned. You may encounter naysayers ready to squash your dream. Start flexing your courage muscle and prepare to stand up and face off against those who disagree with your new path.

There is nothing silly about pursuing a goal that would make your world a better place. Move forward and follow your transformational dream with the creativity and belief of a three-year-old. Be a new you and be remarkable.

# Walk Off a Winner

MY HUSBAND AND I SHARE a passion for baseball. Several years ago, we attended an afternoon game in Anaheim, California, to cheer on the LA Angels. Due to the blazing hot sun, we relinquished our seats near the field in the fourth inning and went off in search of shade. Our body temps refreshed, but the migration did little to boost our morale, as our team was scoreless.

Reflecting on the dismal outlook, I decided there was only one thing under my control: my thought process. Teams come from behind all the time, and I knew a win was possible. As the bottom of the ninth inning commenced, I shot my husband an "oh ye of little faith look," then doubled down and reminded him there is no crying in baseball. I coached him into some positive thinking and set my sights on a walk-off win.

Closing my eyes, I visualized a victory achieved by the trailing Angels resulting in a game over, end of story. Excitement mounted as the team started to rally. What happened next was rather unusual. We accomplished the win and scored at the plate due to a wild pitch.

Yes, I know my positive thinking did not cause the pitcher to fire in a wild one, but it did improve my outlook and made the game more enjoyable. Baseball, like life, is sometimes error-laden. At times we're batting 1,000 and covering all the bases. Then someone throws out a curveball, and we succumb to striking out.

Scoring a walk-off win brings with it not only glory but also a valuable life lesson. Games played on the baseball diamond, or the field of life, aren't won by giving up too soon. Going the distance takes fortitude, perseverance, and the guts to play it out to the last pitch. As so aptly put by baseball icon Yogi Berra, "It ain't over 'til it's over."

At some point, most of us are guilty of giving up on something too soon. Often this is caused by a lack of focus or diminished self-confidence brought on by; you guessed it: stinking thinking. Bombarded by those inner gremlins chattering away in our heads proclaiming it's too hard, we buy into the premise that it's never going to happen. Before long, we've mentally checked out before the final inning.

This week remind yourself that giving up too soon is for losers. Recommit to your most important goal and chase away those nagging negative thoughts. Winners have staying power and sometimes even get a lucky break like an unexpected windfall, or a wild pitch.

# A Ticket to Opportunity

MY FRIEND CAROLYN IS A cautious driver. The only exception occurred many years ago. On that day, Carolyn was pulled over by a local sheriff for exceeding the speed limit. She dutifully accepted a ticket and scheduled traffic school.

While sitting in class several weeks later, my friend felt antsy and bored. The course, designed in a lecture format, was delivered by an instructor who ignored any opportunity to make the material even a bit interesting.

Carolyn drove home, tired, and disappointed. Later that evening, over dinner, she lamented her lackluster experience to husband Michael. It was during that conversation when Carolyn experienced an "aha" moment. She realized Michael, an author, lecturer, and all-around humorous fellow, could breathe life into a traffic class. After all, there is certainly no law against making learning entertaining. That conversation took place over twenty years ago. Since then, Carolyn and Michael have helped ticketed offenders become better drivers while learning in a fun atmosphere.

We cannot prevent unwanted situations from happening, but we can convert the lessons learned into something positive by applying a reframing strategy as Carolyn did. While rewinding the mind-numbing traffic class, my creative friend put her spouse in the picture. She visualized Michael running the program.

The art of reframing experiences may take some practice. The first step is to get rid of any limiting beliefs. For Carolyn, it was easy. She believed traffic school need not be boring and had always admired Michael's gift for making the ordinary something fun and exciting.

Let's make this a little more personal. Imagine vying for a promotion you worked extremely hard to achieve. You feel you deserve it; however, you also know the boss's pet is up for the same opportunity. If you give into stinking thinking; she is the fair-haired child, I don't have a shot at trumping her alliance with him; you create a limiting belief. Power through that crippling thought process and change the picture. Rather than thinking, I'll never, get the promotion, reframe your internal dialogue. Remind yourself of your finely-honed skills and tell yourself repeatedly that you have an excellent chance at it.

Next, think positively and make a physical list of all the reasons why you deserve the promotion. What additional steps can you take to make getting the advancement a reality? If any aspect of your resume requires upgrading, take action. Brush up on a skill; add some self-development to your schedule.

Ready for the final reframing? Utilize visualization techniques. See yourself in the new position. Direct a mental movie of you sitting behind your desk discussing a project with your staff member. Carolyn pictured Michael in the frame as the seminar leader. Follow suit. Nail that promotion by mentally writing your own ticket.

# Humorholic

EVERY YEAR, RIGHT AFTER CHRISTMAS, I hole up in my office, reflecting on the past year and creating my goals for the next twelve months. Wait! Don't stop reading. I'm not going to bore you with what you already know about creating a new year's list of goals. Instead, I'd like to share some information about one item on my list.

For the next 12 months, I'm aspiring to the status of humorholic. (I know it's a word I made up. Sorry spellcheck.) The inspiration came to me by reading a somewhat dated book filled with wisdom. In 1998, humorist Larry Wilde, published *When You're Up to Your Eyeballs in Alligators: How to Use Your Sense of Humor for Unlimited Success, Better Health & Staying Sane When the World Gets a Little Crazy.*

Larry's book regaling the multiple benefits of humor convinced me to develop this skill. We all know that laughter is a timeless wonder drug, but listen up all you people who join a gym, Jenny Craig or Weight Watcher's, every January (all good things of course), Did you know that during a solid belly laugh, we lose 35 calories? Just think if you do that internal jogging brought on by tickling your funny bone 15 times/day, you can burn 525 calories. (As Larry puts it, "You can laugh your ass off.")

Another prominent by-product of humor is enhanced immunity. Scientific evidence indicates there are physical and chemical links between the mind and the immune system. In 2012, studies at Loma Linda University revealed that watching a comedy video strengthens your immune system in measurable ways.

How about reducing your stress level? There is nothing silly about the fact that laughter reduces hormones that cause stress. Perhaps the reason most optimists are healthy is due to a positive state of mind. Optimism keeps healthy people well and speeds up the recovery process in those who are ill.

For those of you placing extra focus on your career in the coming year, note that a study done by executive recruiting firm Robert Half International revealed individuals with a sense of humor do better at their jobs than those with little or no working funny bone. Want to get that promotion? In addition to all your hard work, try making the boss and your peers laugh more.

Lastly, don't be afraid to laugh at yourself. (Being blonde, that one's a no-brainer for me.) Self-deprecating humor is a powerful force in bonding with others.

So, if you're convinced becoming a humorholic will improve many areas of your life, add it to your list just like I did.

# Lemonade in a Box

RECENTLY I READ A STORY about a dad cleaning out the garage with his five-year-old daughter. When they came across a large brown cardboard square, he saw a box. His daughter squealed with delight. Why? She visualized a lemonade stand! Together they turned her active imagination into reality. The next day the little girl set up shop serving ice-cold lemonade to neighbors and anyone who happened through the community. You can imagine her pride at the end of the workday when she smiled up at her dad, displaying a total of $27.12, stored in a shoebox.

The lesson lingered with me for days. It is so natural for children to think outside the box (pun intended), but sometimes, creative thinking is difficult for adults. We all possess the ability to innovate. Sometimes inventiveness hides beneath the surface, giving us the impression we have lost the ability.

When was the last time you let your imagination soar? What month or year was it when you broke the rules and did the unthinkable? Tap into your memory and conjure up your most creative project. Remember feeling the joy of breaking the boundaries? Drawing out your inner optimist is the trick to creativity. Don't fret anticipating the outcome; just let go and have fun.

Much like a runner preparing for a marathon, you can get in the zone by employing some warm-up strategies. Music can stimulate your creative genes. Do what Einstein did, listen to Mozart. Or, tune in to some good old rock and roll if that is your preference. Tap into nature by lacing up your hiking boots and hitting a scenic trail to release endorphins. Maybe a quiet stroll in the park strikes your fancy? Stimulate your mind by doing crosswords or a puzzle.

Once you've done your warm-up, relax. Let the new ideas percolate up to the surface. Are you starting to feel that creative spark? Write all your thoughts down. Don't strive for perfection. Brainstorm and have fun with it.

What's next? Action! Pour out your inspiration into a project. Start that children's book you always wanted to write, or hit the craft store for art supplies and begin to paint your masterpiece. Create and compile a book of poems, sign up for piano lessons, or enroll in a drama class.

Continue to develop your inventive side. Make it a habit to unleash your creativity often. By doing so, I promise you the next time you view a brown cardboard square, you will NOT see a box. Now, let's go make some lemonade!

# Sunny Your Brain

My friend David is a hoot! He has a quiz addiction. The other day David stated a quiz declared him a member of the obsessive-compulsive disorder tribe. No gray areas, he scored 100%. We lovingly teased him. It was unnecessary to take a quiz to learn what we all knew to be true.

Rarely do I get sucked up into quiz mania, but today I stopped mid-page in an old "Success Magazine" to test my score on "The Optimism Quiz," a short test by David Mezzapelle, author of the *Contagious Optimism* book series. According to Mezzapelle, individuals whose results fall in the range of 37 – 50 are optimists possessing "strong positive qualities including gratitude, hope, altruism, and persistence." My score was 45. On a bit of a roll (David would be proud), I took another short personality test revealing the same results.

Doing a deeper dive into the subject of optimism, I did some research. The first thing I wanted to know was; am I a natural-born optimist, or did I learn it. My findings reported genetics do play a minor role, approximately 20%. It made sense to me that I inherited some of those genes, as my positive-thinking mother was indeed a glass half full person.

Optimists experience physical benefits, according to Dr. Martin Seligman, often referred to as the father of positive psychology. The good doctor claims optimism improves the immune system, prevents chronic disease, and aids individuals in coping with adverse events.

No one is exempt from stressful situations, and there is no magic formula that makes feelings of anxiety disappear. However, individuals with positive-thinking traits process stressful events differently. Studies show an optimistic person typically recovers faster from nasty set-backs.

If you feel you are more of a realist, the highly pragmatic type, or even a glass half empty type person, Seligman, who authored the book, *Learned Optimism: How to Change Your Life and Mind*, believes, you can change behaviors. In the book, he delivers techniques that make use of what he calls "learned optimism."

Cognitive psychologist Elaine Fox, author of *Rainy Brain, Sunny Brain: How to Retrain Your Brain to Overcome Pessimism and Achieve a More Positive Outlook*, agrees we can learn to adopt an optimistic demeanor.

Whether you are a pessimist, realist, or high on the optimist spectrum, the bottom line is a little positive thinking can help you maneuver through life's roadblocks. This week, challenge yourself to find the break in the clouds and see if, by doing so, your stress level lessens.

# Optimism

IN SUMMARY:

- Reframe the situation
- Ignite your imagination
- Ignore the naysayers
- Laugh at yourself
- Break the boundaries
- Brainstorm
- Linger in positive moments
- Don't give up

# Procrastination
# Eliminate Wasted
# Moments

"Someday is not a day of the week."

— JANET DAILEY

# Lose the Snooze

EMILY RUSHED INTO MY OFFICE a full fifteen minutes late for our appointment. Keeping my face passive, I did a mental eye roll. This was session number three, and my client arrived late each time. Beyond being disrespectful to my schedule, this was symptomatic of an issue we addressed involving Emily's lack of productivity.

Upon inquiring why Emily was tardy, I discovered the root cause, namely her snooze button. Full disclosure: I harbor strong feelings regarding snooze buttons and chewing gum; my position is both should be outlawed. (If you've ever unknowingly stepped in a nasty wad of bubble gum or ruined a great pair of jeans by sitting in a theater seat where the gooey substance hid, you might agree.)

My feud with the snoozer tab is it allows delays and is the precursor to a harmful habit. Hitting that button is permitting yourself to postpone the inevitable. We start the day behind and race the clock. If the day begins in that manner, rarely, if ever, do we catch up.

In her book, *Stop Saying You're Fine: The No BS Guide to Getting What You Want*, life coach, author, and CNN commentator Mel Robbins, proclaims, "When you hit the snooze button you surrender power." I fully agree the snooze button is our worst enemy. Delaying any action to accomplish our dreams places us stuck in a world of unhappiness. Giving into resistance only gets us to nowheresville.

Robbins recommends a solution to combat our lazy desire to resist action, which she dubs the "five-second rule." The premise is if you wait longer than five seconds to take action, your good intention will melt. This tactic worked for me. Although I have no problem getting out of bed, I admit to pushing my internal snooze button when it's time to hit the gym. The next day when my brain signaled gym time, I immediately changed into my workout clothes and headed out the door. That's the trick. Do NOT give yourself a five-second delay, take control, and execute your action item.

During my session with Emily, we discussed how she sabotages her goals by delaying action and staying stuck. She agreed to toss out her alarm clock, the one with the snooze button, and guess what? The following week Emily proudly waltzed in my office with five minutes to spare. Thanks to Mel's strategy, she produced a list of accomplishments attributed to employing the five-second rule.

# Dragging My Feet

YESTERDAY PROCRASTINATION BIT ME BIG time. I dreaded starting a particular project. It wasn't a distasteful task (a friend asked me to write a guest blog for her website), but I was rebellious about beginning. Cleaning the grill, scrubbing down the shower tiles, even cleaning out the fish tank (not that we have one) sounded more appealing.

How do you solve a case of the blahs about attacking a particular task? At a loss, I turned to my friend Google for an answer. When all else fails, ask the experts. There must be 365 ways to beat procrastination, right?

Diving into my research, I spied an appealing approach. Number three on a post of 11 was, "Jump right in, no matter what." That may sound counterintuitive when you're procrastinating. Well, I promised myself if I "jumped in' and made one small step on the project, I would let myself off the hook for at least 20 minutes. Done. Although I struggled, I composed the first three paragraphs of the blog.

As I returned to my research, another tidbit resonated. "Work in the right environment." I was in my office, an ideal setting for writing; however, the overtones of the ballgame my husband was watching filtered throughout the house. To top it off, my guy cannot view a game without shouting out advice to the batter or berating the umpire over a rotten call. Packing up my laptop, I reconvened to the peaceful patio where I worked for a while until I was distracted by a couple of rabbits engaging in what looked like a game of tag.

Completing only two more paragraphs wasn't progress, so I returned to the drawing board with a sense of urgency. Another expert suggested I take a break to complete another more palatable item on my to-do list. Why? Mr. Expert claimed accomplishing something would provide the momentum needed to work in earnest on the primary task. Having the ideal job in mind, I returned to the house and slowly folded a massive laundry load. Relaxing into the task, I allowed my mind to get creative about the message I wanted to convey in the blog. I poured myself a glass of lemonade, returned to the patio, and spent the next 40 minutes polishing off the blog.

My take-away from the bout with procrastination is two-fold. Number one, forgive yourself. We all slip up and succumb to dragging our feet on a project. Number two, let procrastination work for you. If I hadn't taken a break, my laundry would still be in a large pile.

It seems to me there is never one cure-all, so next time procrastination gets the better of you, start the task, change your environment, take a break, and then get the job done. It worked for me.

# Clutter Makes You Fat

Did you know that in 95% of Japanese schools, there's no need for a janitor? It's true. I watched a video clip on the subject worth mentioning. In Japan, students clean their classrooms every day. Educators believe this teaches them humility, modesty, and teamwork. No wonder Japan ranks as the world's cleanest country.

I tell you this to draw a parallel. The benefits of cleaning a schoolroom are akin to putting a little spit and polish on your work or home office. It should come as no surprise that streamlining your workspace can bolster your productivity. I'm not going to tell you how to set up a tidy desk area. If you need help, check with the international expert Marie Kond , author of the best-seller book, *The Life Changing Magic of Tidying Up: The Japanese Art of Decluttering and Organizing.*

We feel more at peace and put together when both our home and our minds are uncluttered. According to Psychology Today, science can prove keeping your environment neat and organized is highly beneficial. Research scientists at Indiana University found that people with clean houses are healthier than individuals with messy homes.

Leave it to Princeton University to discover it's all about the brain. Ready for the geeky stuff? Their findings indicated; "The visual cortex could be overwhelmed by task-irrelevant objects (what we might term clutter on our desktop), making it difficult to allocate attention to the task at hand and complete it efficiently."

What about the association of clutter and memory loss? Research supports that one too. According to studies done by Lynn Hasher at the University of Toronto, material clogging up your neural networks slows you down, making you less efficient in processing information. This can result in your short-term memory's incapacitation, causing you to forget the information you should know.

Think food and clutter are related? Here's a fun fact. A joint United States and Australian study showed people eat more snacks and cookies if the environment is chaotic.

Have I convinced you to get out that trash bag and start streamlining your environment? Oh, and remember, clutter can be physical or virtual. One glance at my phone text messages and email inbox signals I have some massive purging to do.

So stop procrastinating and start today; make it a point to purge and clean. Not only will you be pleased with your surroundings, but your mental acuity will also improve, and who doesn't need a little sharpening of the gray matter?

# Out of the Closet

WHILE UNPACKING MY BAGS AFTER a lovely beach vacation, I opened a closet to put away some belongings. The joyful, carefree mood I carried back from the coast instantly evaporated as I viewed the tangled mess of shoes and disorganized clothing. When did this happen, I wondered? Normally I maintain a wardrobe with clean, pressed garments arranged in color hues hanging neatly in the walk-in while shoes obediently sit below in tidy rows. Oh, who am I kidding? I had no reason for fake surprise. I've been procrastinating over organizing that closet for several months.

The word procrastination stuck in my craw like the stray sandal I discovered wedged between a pair of black pumps. Typically I am not prone to delaying action items on my to-do list. Scrolling through my memory of months past, I realized it took me forever this year to organize tax documents for the accountant. Several other recent instances came to mind where chores remained undone until the eleventh hour.

As a career coach, I realized the need to do some heavy-duty self-coaching before the procrastination habit adhered to me like duct tape on a leaky beach ball. My concern was not why I recently fell behind. I'm human and occasionally succumb to bouts of rebellious laziness. My sole interest was instituting the fix.

I immediately invoked the ten-minute rule. Experts at "Psychology Today" recommend a "five-minute rule," but I knew 300 seconds wasn't going to cut it. I positioned the timer and spent the full ten bringing some semblance of order to the wayward shoe jumble. Feeling a bit better about the closet fiasco, I knew the next step was setting a completion date. I reviewed my schedule for Monday and slotted in another 45 minutes to complete the job. Knowing that carrot motivation works better than the stick, I promised myself when the wardrobe reflected proper order; I'd treat myself to a new beach cover-up AFTER I compiled a stack of gently used items and dropped them off in a downtown donation box. Had I resorted to self-bribery? You bet, but for a good cause. Not only that, but good behavior also deserves a reward, right?

Are you blatantly ignoring a chore? Make time to tackle the job, even if it is just ten minutes a day. Reframe the outcome and sweeten the pie. Organizing the overloaded and unkempt garage means you could hold a garage sale. Just think what you could do with the proceeds!

# Thanks to Sir Newton

EVER FEEL STUCK? YOU WANT to get things done, but perhaps don't know where to begin, so you remain in a limbo-like stupor. Sure, we've all experienced living in the status quo's land, dreaming big dreams, but taking no action. Fear not because stagnation is only temporary. One simple key to accomplishing your goals is to establish some momentum.

Recently I watched a rather mundane video about momentum. I knew I'd never make it through nine minutes and ten seconds of blah, blah, blah, but two minutes into the film, my ears perked up as I considered this little physics lesson. Newton's First Law, "An object at rest stays at rest, and an object in motion stays in motion with the same speed unless acted upon by an unbalanced force." That was all I needed to hear. After all, it's a law, right? Just focusing on it gave me a well-needed boost, and I was off and running propelled by the fact that nothing would happen if I didn't move.

I like to think it's all about the little things, so it's okay to start small. There is power in taking baby steps and accomplishing a two-minute task. Why? Because checking something off your do-to list, however, small elicits a sense of accomplishment. Making that checkmark signals completion of an action item.

Momentum builds, encouraging you to move on to more significant work.

Want more? Start by shaking up your routine. Yes, you do need a process, a way to get work done, but sometimes we get too bogged down in our day-to-day systematic way of going about business. When you get creative and step outside your hum-drum routine, you'll begin to feel inspired. A new way of doing things spurs momentum and Newton's rule about being and staying in motion kicks in.

If the change in routine doesn't get you on a forward projectile, you may need some inspiration. Just reading Newton's law was like a kick in the pants for me, but if that leaves you cold, look elsewhere. Read a motivational blog, find a quote that rings true, or compose an affirmation that spurs you to action.

Need more to fuel your fire? Find an accountability partner, hire a coach, or turn to technology. Numerous apps like https://www.goalsontrack.com/ (which is free) help you plan and track your goals. With an app called https://lifetick.com/, those who hold you accountable can view your progress on goals and cheer you on.

Utilize whatever strategy appeals to you. Think about how much you can get done this week once you begin! Stop making excuses and get moving now. Make your best kick-in-the-pants move, and keep the momentum going.

# Procrastination

IN SUMMARY:

- Streamline your environment
- Jump into a task
- Change your environment
- Lose the snooze
- Employ the five-second rule
- Set a ten-minute timer
- Reward yourself
- Take baby steps
- Get an accountability partner

# Organization
# Cultivate Essential
# Habits

"Organizing is what you do before you do something,
so that when you do it, it is not all mixed up"

— A. A. MILNE

# Out of Office

STOPPING FOR A MOMENT TO put down my summer beach read and rest my eyes, I scanned the activity around the resort's Olympic sized pool. Some inhabitants stretched out on the luxurious beach chairs were contently soaking up the sun; others, like me, engaged in light reading. I sighed, observing about a third of the vacationers intently working their notebooks and cell phones. As I strolled to the Tiki Bar for an icy Mojito, it did not surprise me to catch snippets of business-related conversations.

Full disclosure, in the past, I have been guilty of checking my work voice mails and emails but wised-up. I began to wonder if my action was ego-driven. Did I think the team back home couldn't exist without me? Or, perhaps, was I insecure and feeling left out of important decisions. So I would call in and retrieve news from the office, but, admittedly, it took me at least an hour to stop thinking about the work piling up on my desk. My husband keyed in on my distraction and sooner or later delivered his "why are we on vacation if you are going to engage the office from afar", speech. Yep...busted!

Taking 15 minutes a day to check in with the office doesn't sound harmful, but beware, it's a trap--the time you spend thinking about work after your innocent check-in robs your peace.

Without a solid turn-off switch, thoughts of sales contracts, employee issues, and the marketing proposal you need to write upon your return start bouncing around in your brain.

A real vacation occurs when you leave an "out of the office" message on your voice mail greeting and email. No, it's not impossible. Crazy as it sounds, you can convince yourself there is no requirement to check-in. Your only job on vacation is to take a break from work pressures and have fun. The whole idea of taking time off is to return to work refreshed and recharged.

If you want the ultimate benefit of a vacation from work, go off the grid. Leave your cell phone at home. Want to capture the beauty of that exotic place you dreamt of while sitting in your cubicle pinning for an escape, then bring a camera. If you are addicted to informing all your Facebook friends of your vacation, you can post when you return. Give it a try. Keep your time away from the office sacred. You'll be glad you did!

# Trash Your To-Do List?

IN OUR FAST-PACED, OFTEN CHAOTIC world, we continually strive
for efficiency and productivity. I am fascinated with any system
or product that helps me manage time and clutter. Organizing
tools are my favorite purchases. While my female peers are enam-
ored with stylish shoe boutiques, my "go-to" retail outlet is The
Container Store. I own sock beds, spice racks, hanging jewelry
storage contraptions, car caddy containers, color-coded file fold-
ers, and an assortment of padded and multiple tiered hangers.

In addition to organizational products, I inhale every article
that promises to take me to the next level of minimizing clutter and becoming more productive. Having solemn respect for
inventorying action items, I carry my to-do list around like a
small child totes his favorite worn-out teddy bear. I admit to feeling a little high each time I cross an item off my never-ending
register of yet to be accomplished tasks.

Obsessed with productivity hacks, I recently read a blog professing the value of creating a "done list," which is the flip side
of our traditional to-do. Reading this counterintuitive theory
was like turning the shower setting to frigid and remaining
under the icy current until I turned purple. For years I believed

every efficiency expert's sage advice; list your goals and all steps needed to get there.

Asking me to part with daily to-do's is akin to demanding a toddler turn in his "binky." Reluctantly, I decided to give it a go for a week. Knowing it was impossible to go cold-turkey, I struck a deal with myself. I alternated days between working on my "to do" and "done list." Days spent in the done-mode meant recording any meaningful wins. Each evening I was to reflect on and celebrate my accomplishments. I must admit feeling some satisfaction in the review process. Could it be possible that a "done list" is a motivational tool? Mind you, some days were frustrating. I did not accomplish nearly as much as I wanted. Remaining faithful to the instructions in the blog, I spent time analyzing my setbacks. Part of the exercise is jotting down observations and working out the kinks.

At the end of my experimental week, I would have to say the jury is still out. I doubt I'll ever fully kick the habit of creating to-do's, but sincerely acknowledge the done list's benefits.

Give it a try and see which method works best to help you create a balanced perspective and a more productive life. Finding the right organizational system is always a win!

# Advice From The Guru

IT HAPPENS EVERY JANUARY. A few weeks after packing the holiday decorations away, I develop an urge to streamline my life, beginning with the clutter hiding behind the scenes. My home and office appear pristine and streamlined on the surface, but cabinets and closets sometimes hold a challenging assignment for an organizational expert.

Intent on never having to repeat the cycle, I decided to find a once-and-for-all system. My strategy was to seek advice from the Japanese cleaning consultant, Marie Kondo, dubbed the "Guru of Tidiness." I read that the author of *The Life-Changing Magic of Tidying Up* has clients lined-up on a three-month waiting list. Wow! I plunked down my $16.99 plus tax and dove into this New York Times bestseller.

The book helped diagnose my problem. I possess a fear of letting go of certain items like books (even my Kindle is on overload) and my nemesis, magazines. I confess to being a magazine maniac--the kind you can hold in your hand and admire the glossy photos. My library includes subscriptions to everything from "Success" to "Southern Living". Since I do not have the time to read them all, these periodicals fill my cabinets and closets and are probably lurking in the garage boxes. And yes, no matter how much I thin my wardrobe each season, I still have too many clothes.

Kondo professes, "When we delve into the reasons why we cannot let something go, there are only two: an attachment to the past or a fear of the future." So I searched my soul and found nothing to fear. Then I launched a campaign to sort items into multiple containers for pitching and donating. Marie was 100% accurate about reducing what we own. Streamlining is essentially detoxing our home, and the detox has a positive effect on our well-being.

Where is your clutter? Is it in piles of reading material, or multiple pairs of shoes you never wear loitering in boxes beneath your bed? Still hanging on to that outdated blazer in your closet or the ugly sweater Aunt Sarah gave you for Christmas five years ago? What is this intense connection we have with material objects that serve no purpose?

Feel like joining me in this? Let's all experience a mental uplift by freeing up space in our offices, garages, and psyches. I'm saying goodbye to Martha Stewart Living, July 2009. How about you throw out those sexy red stilettos that make your feet hurt within five minutes of wear? Put your surrounding environment in order. Keep what brings you joy. My new mantra is clear your space and clear your mind.

# Taking Back Control

A QUOTE ATTRIBUTED TO ARISTOTLE I always find motivating is, "Well begun is half done." I don't know if I dare claim "well begun," however, this weekend, my husband and I did make a minor dent in clearing the clutter from our garage. Not an easy feat. It took us a week to agree on a date to begin purging the many years of accumulated items we forgot we even owned. We can place the blame of tackling this long overdue task on laziness, but digging a little deeper reveals fear, uncertainty, and a splash of sadness.

Why fear? It is probably common to hold onto things for that one "someday" when we might need it. We might be reluctant to let go of an item purchased with our hard-earned money as it signals wastefulness. Indeed John and I found ourselves remiss to toss items conjuring up sweet and romantic memories of our long-term relationship; in fact, we had to save that purge for another round.

Decluttering isn't just about making a neat and organized garage to house gardening supplies, tools, and holiday decorations. It goes far beyond carefully labeling and lining up matching bins making the space look like an ad in "Good Housekeeping Magazine" for The Container Store. No, for many, myself included, ridding an area of the office or home of unused, unwanted belongings supports a desire to simplify life.

According to June Saruwatari, author of the book, *Beyond the Clutter,* staying in front of the curve on chaos and unfinished projects "keeps your mind from going haywire." The author advises if you begin storing piles of items in a closet, you can shut the door; however, "you still carry it with you." A key question to ponder is how many items must you hold onto before these belongings begin to control your life.

At the end of the allotted time spent in the garage, John and I smiled happily over what we accomplished. Following the words of experts like Saruwatari, the next step is to get ruthless about taking actions to eliminate the stuck energy existing in physical spaces packed with possessions, no longer serving a purpose.

How about it? Ready to eliminate all the unnecessary stuff in your life? You'll have more time for yourself, less responsibility, and an enhanced view as you gaze around your environment. Let's make a pact to kick the clutter to the curb together and take control of our space.

I challenge you to inventory areas of your home and your personal life littered with items and activities no longer joyful or useful. Call it spring-cleaning or the path to simplification and repeat after me: "Well begun is half done."

# Organization

In Summary:

* Eliminate unwanted clutter
* Adopt "out of office"
* Start spring cleaning
* Select an organizational tool
* Commit to letting go

# Blues Busters
# Combating the Enemy

"You cannot always control what goes on outside.
But you can always control what goes on inside"

— WAYNE DYER

# How a Good Girl Steps Out of Line

It is no surprise to those who know me that I fall into the "goody-two-shoes" category. If you've never met me, take my word for it because part of my persona is sticking to the truth. I've never gotten a traffic ticket, ignored a jury duty summons, or neglected to return my library books by the due date. I do have one naughty little secret to share with you; I play hooky. Not only do I believe in escaping from where the world expects you to be on a given day, I highly recommend it.

Call it a mental health day, a Ferris Bueller lark, or designated "me time," refer to it by whatever name you choose, but do not deny yourself the occasional escape from your many obligations and duties.

Before you go too far off the beaten path, the good girl side of me must warn you about the rules. Granted, they are my rules, but I hope you will indulge me. First, understand that hooky is a special dispensation granted to the worn-out deserving inner you. It should not be abused or turned into a habit. I allow myself one day per year. My second rule is to choose the day wisely. Careful planning is necessary so that innocent people don't suffer as a result of your absence. For example, do not take personal time from work on a day an important project is due, renege on playing teacher's helper the morning of your third grader's field trip or cancel out an hour before your mother-in-law's big birthday bash.

The third and most important rule, do something that gives you great joy. Escape to the beach with a picnic lunch or hide out in the library and lose yourself in a racy novel. Check into a day spa, go fishing, or drive to the city and play tourist. Feel like bolting the doors and keeping the world at bay? It's okay to stay home and binge on Netflix. Watch the daytime soaps (if you must) and sip on a Mimosa while soaking in the tub. The point of this day of freedom is to recharge and refresh.

One last rule: banish any thoughts of guilt from your mind. Hooky is an annual event (by my standards) strategically planned to deviate from the norm. The sole purpose is to relieve stress and prevent burn-out. It is a day of freedom rich with the significant benefit of blissful peace. Experience the joy and then return to your routine a happier you!

# Stress Journaling

Whenever Carmen walks in my office, the first thing she does is produce her constant companion, her journal, and bring me up to date on what transpired since our last session. I admired my client's dedication to journaling. The process of chronicling her thoughts and insights on daily happenings works well for her.

People journal for various reasons, ranging from improving focus and mental clarity to experiencing a sense of accomplishment in recording achievements. I rarely recommend journaling to my clients, although I probably should. It can be a viable stress reliever and useful in catching insightful thoughts and creative ideas, but frankly, journaling is not my thing. Why don't I journal? It's a process I don't enjoy. Suffice it to say, different strokes. What works for Carmen doesn't necessarily work for me.

But keep reading, as I do have one crucial singular exception to my journaling outlook. You can journal whenever you like, or not, but when a stressful situation results in a multitude of negative thoughts bouncing around in your brain, I recommend you sit in a quiet place and take pen to paper or tap away at your keyboard.

According to studies at UCLA, when participants wrote down their negative emotions, versus verbalizing, activity in the brain's alarm center (called the amygdala) decreased. In layman's terms, brain scans proved committing your feelings in writing stopped the madness. Once you quiet those antagonistic scenes lurking in your mind, tranquility sets in, and you can calmly begin to work out the problem that had you ricocheting off the walls.

Stop and think of a time when a stressful experience occurred, and you handled it poorly. No doubt, you stayed inside your head and held dark thoughts captive. Without a pathway to clear those pessimistic feelings, you ended up reacting to emotion and making poor decisions. Perhaps you blurted out things you regret or acted impulsively.

Of course, it's too late to rewind what's said and done, but never too late to employ this particular journaling strategy. The next time you feel overwhelmed by a boatload of stress, take a time out to steal away and capture all the pent up negativity on paper. Do so without judging, and refrain from editing. Remember, this is for your eyes only. Write until you feel empty of all those distressing thoughts. Then take some cleansing breaths and calm yourself. At that point, you will be able to rationally and successfully deal with the issue.

# Time to Escape

THE OTHER DAY WHILE PERUSING social media, I spotted a picture of a little boy lying across a playground swing with his tiny legs dangling. The caption read, "Not a care in the world." He was hanging out, staring at an anthill, or thinking about being an astronaut or maybe an upcoming Disneyland trip. Studying the shot gave me a sense of peace. It depicted life, as we wish it, no worries, just pure contentment.

As we journey into adulthood, the phrase, not a care in the world, probably isn't the best descriptor of our current state of mind. Let's face it; adulting is hard work because growing up is a process that heaps layers of responsibility upon our lives. We transition from being dependent to self-assertive, which means stepping up, taking control, and being accountable.

We all have days when we want to chuck the notion of acting like a grownup and revert to living a carefree life. Ever feel like studying anthills from a playground swing might be a delightful diversion from your overtaxed, over-scheduled, overspent life? Yeah, me too. When I start feeling I'm totally over everything, I know the problem. Those symptoms are indicative of a person in need of a vacation.

A volume of scientific evidence exists on the necessity of breaking from daily life rigors to benefit from time off. Some people prefer taking one massive vacation, which is excellent, but I lace my calendar with more short-term holidays. Studies show we experience a boost in happiness before and after a vacation. So the more holidays I take, the happier I get.

Beyond the happiness factor, there are multiple other reasons to take vacations. One somewhat out-of-the-box theory I researched is weight loss. Often people who are stressed engage in mindless eating. Also, the stress hormone, cortisol, is linked to increased belly fat and weight gain. Vacationing your stress and fat cells away is a happy thought, right?

As one of the world's worst sleepers (yes, I totally suck at sleeping), my favorite benefit involves getting some quality shut-eye. Researchers report vacationers experience an improved quality of sleep both while on holiday and after returning home.

Another benefit is the bonding factor. Whether you're vacationing with your family or a group of friends, vacations help people relax and enjoy making memories together. If you're thinking about pushing back, claiming you cannot afford the time off, forget it. I'm not taking no for an answer. Get creative and figure out a way to break away, if only for a day or two.

So this weekend I am taking my own advice. If anyone wants me, I'll be at my happy place, the beach, getting skinny, and indulging in a few good night sleeps.

# Bless Me, Father, For I'm a Dad

As I was completing my last coaching session of the week, I cheerfully wished my client a Happy Father's Day. Unknowingly I had figuratively stepped on a land mine. He scoffed after a long and lengthy sigh, telling me his dream day included a juicy steak and a nap in a hammock situated somewhere in a breezy leafy green. Ivan then explained due to the dynamics of a modern blended family, the special day America sets aside to honor dads would find him shuttling around town from one clan gathering to another. He feared the menu on the stressful day would consist of hot dogs, overtired and cranky children, and a significant amount of windshield time.

Described like that, it sounded like penance. I did a mental eye roll. He was a hard-working guy and certainly deserved an extended lounge in the hammock and a prime porterhouse. However, my job was not to offer condolences but to use this as an opportunity for a coaching moment.

Based on Ivan's tone, I knew he would approach the undesirable plans with a "grin and bear it" attitude. Indeed, the act of enduring an event by faking good humor is one approach to get him through the day. A more positive method of dealing with any unwanted situation is to put some sincere effort into reframing it. Knowing Ivan is a family man who truly loves his wife and kids gave me an idea. I suggested that car rides could be fun if some simple planning went into it.

Involving the children in a road trip game, planning silly jokes or singing contests laced with mandatory short bouts of quiet time as the children mentally prepared for the next challenge or resorted to downtime with their kiddy electronics could make the excursion enjoyable. Ivan and his wife might entertain the troops regaling stories of their youth. Kids might find it fascinating to learn before the birth of the Leapfrog Leappad, MP3 players, and radio-controlled robots their parents entertained themselves with Rubik cubes, hula-hoops, or a game of dodge ball.

My client began to get the idea and started to warm up to the subject. A small smile lingered on his face as he reflected on his coveted Matchbox car collection. He added some of his ideas to make the car ride fun.

I still wanted to see him get that steak, so I recommended getting a sitter and planning a date night with his wife during the week. As my dear old dad would have proclaimed, now we were cooking with gas.

# Riding Regrets

EVER SUFFERED ONE OF THOSE bleak, black Mondays? I did recently. Despite my best-laid plans, I made a lousy decision. Unfortunately, it wasn't until Tuesday afternoon that I realized I'd spent the entire morning worrying and regretting the previous day's happenings. Immediately I began to talk myself out of a negative reverie. Not only was I practicing poor time management, ruminating was accomplishing nothing. I needed to stop stressing over yesterday and be a little kinder to myself.

Regret is a part of life. We don't get it right every time and consequently end up bemoaning our decisions, actions, and often our words. Hours spent lamenting cannot change the past. The fact is, life is not a dress rehearsal equipped with do-overs. Our only choice is to dispense with the "should haves" and move on.

By that evening, as the desert moon cast it's beams over the earth, I mentally waved good-bye to any remaining regrets lingering in deep in the corners of my mind. After using a trusted process to banish my woes, I transitioned into a positive mode by utilizing a simple two-step process.

First, analyze what went wrong. If you dig deep enough, you can probably come up with multiple reasons. In my case, by attempting to hasten the decision-making process, I omitted extensive research. As I called myself out for moving too fast, an old Yiddish proverb came to mind: "Measure ten times and cut once," Grabbing a marker, I wrote it out and posted it on my vision board. If I was going to learn from this, I needed to keep it in front of me.

Next, practicing kindness, I forgave myself. Sure, it took some self-talk, as I was disappointed in myself. I'm aware from experience if I muster up enough fortitude, I can push through it. Assuring myself, it wasn't the first error I made, and it wasn't fatal. I moved on and refocused my energy on accomplishing an essential item on my to-do list. Getting a task completed is uplifting and served to recharge my confidence level.

The next time you find yourself stressing over a stumble, use the situation to rebuild. Take the time to determine where you went off course and treat yourself gently. One last thought, and Kelly Clarkson sings about it. "What doesn't kill you makes you stronger." So suck it up and walk a little taller.

# Dialing Down

How do you dial down your intensity level? A client posed that question during a recent coaching session. His query made sense. When I met him two years ago, it did not take long to realize Mitch possessed a fierce drive to succeed.

One definition of intensity is a high or extreme degree of emotional excitement. The word also means "the fire you draw on when you are dealing with heightened circumstances." No matter how you describe this high-spirited personality characteristic, it is the degree of intensity that can catapult you to great achievements or inhibit your ability to work harmoniously with others.

Perhaps you have encountered or even worked for a demanding boss known for delivering harsh rebukes and tossing humiliating comments at others. An unchecked intensity such as this demoralizes others and conjures up negative feelings proving, that a highly emotional reaction to an intense desire to achieve is destructive.

My client admitted he had a habit of mowing down anyone in the way of progress. Recognizing the need to change, he valued learning to control his temper and his, my way or the highway ultimatums. So, for my intense client and others who share the same characteristics, the question is, how do we apply the brakes and become a sea of calm when our insides are raging?

Multiple strategies begin with the tried and true numbers game, counting to 10. My personal go-to is a walk-about. If possible, do that physically by briefly excusing yourself, postponing a discussion, or just mentally taking a time out. Once you eject yourself from a situation driven by your escalating intensity, practice some relaxation techniques. Try doing a deep breathing regimen to attain a state of tranquility.

One expert recommends a technique that might stop you cold. As your intensity escalates, visualize a nearby camera getting ready to film your reaction and broadcast it to the world. It might be somewhat embarrassing, right? Keep that one in mind.

When you begin to feel relaxed, get analytical, and zero in on what triggered your strong feelings. Take a moment to examine the consequences of forging ahead full stream versus employing a little consideration for the opposition you were about to crush. Ask yourself how important this will be in the long run. Does the situation warrant a level of aggressive action, or can you bring it down a notch and accomplish the goal without shattering relationships and burning bridges?

A final suggestion, accept the fact that not everyone drives at mega speed. There is a difference between compromising your intention and lightening up a bit. Try it. The results of less stress and increased harmony may surprise you.

# Dr. Seuss is My Go To

I AWOKE BEFORE DAWN, TROUBLED by a disturbing nightmare. Upset and wide awake, I roamed around the house in the dark, thinking if I moved away from the bedroom, dream remnants could not pursue me. I was wrong. Not only did they latch on to me during the early morning hours, the dream demons continued to haunt me.

I had a hard time believing I could not shake the troubling scenes that rattled me awake hours before, but then a thought occurred to me. In my coaching practice, I teach others that we are in charge of our thoughts. It was time to start walking my talk. Surely I could evict those ominous, uninvited, and unwanted visitors camped inside my head, and eventually, I did.

Occasionally, if we are under stress, we all succumb to a bout with the blues. What actions should you take when something dissolves your sunny disposition into a stormy status? Let me walk you through some strategies.

Change your environment. Check. I left the room. It was a good start, but rather unsuccessful. Next, I changed my focus. Entering my office, I began to push away the dark clouds fogging my brain by centering my attention on what needed accomplishing. Okay, this gave me some relief; however, there were recurring moments when the gloomy dark dream surfaced like a jack-in-the-box when the lid pops off.

One of my favorite strategies is "hitting the delete button." I visualized a remote in my hand and watched as I pressed delete, signaling my brain to cancel those dream demons. Next, I moved on to "changing the channel." which brings me to another very successful approach. Using a tactic discussed by Dr. Simone Ravicz in her book, *Brain Boosters: Seven Ways to Help Your Brain Help Yourself* I opted for "savoring." I replaced my negative thoughts giving concerted attention to a recent pleasant experience. Aha! Before long, I felt peaceful. As a brain coach Dr. Ravicz explains it technically, but I think it has something to do with my neurons firing and being wired together over a pleasant memory that helped blank out the blues.

Here are a few more suggestions. A natural remedy lies right outside our door. Want to increase the production of serotonin in your brain? Banish your stress by stepping out into nature. Another go-to is phone a friend. Connecting with others is a quick and easy way to break away from feelings of sadness.

My last suggestion is ideal if you're stuck indoors, and your friends are unavailable. Do you have a favorite book from your childhood? If it's not something you held onto, do a search and download a blues-buster book that gets you to your happy place. For me, it's anything written by Dr. Seuss. Who can't resist those wacky, upbeat rhymes like, *"Congratulations! Today is your day. You're off to Great Places. You're off and away."*

Feeling better now? You deserve to be happy. Embrace that thought!

# Blues Busters

IN SUMMARY:

* Count to ten
* Take a time out
* Lighten up
* Change your focus
* Hit the delete button
* Go outside
* Play hooky
* Forgive yourself
* Journal
* Take cleansing breaths
* Take a vacation

# Success
# Trail to Triumph

"I failed my way to success."

— THOMAS EDISON

# Change Your Label, Change Your Life

RECENTLY I CLICKED ON AN interesting blog about a young man who, at the age of fourteen, set a goal of getting straight A's throughout high school. It sounded like an admirable achievement, so I read on to learn his strategy.

Steven attained success by employing two distinct methodologies. After considerable research and reflection of his past grades, he discovered students who earn lower grades apply last-minute study habits. Attempting to tackle assignments at the eleventh hour adds an element of pressure. Kids who do so often end up frazzled and tired when sitting for an exam. What is key to an "A" student's approach is immediate learning and processing of new information.

Okay, that's not rocket science. Anyone who has ever popped No-Doz and pulled an all-nighter can testify to the stupidity of the process. Sure, you may end up passing with a mediocre grade, but studies performed at UCLA claim inadequate sleep patterns cause a compounded issue. Habits of cramming and sleep deprivation result in more significant academic problems.

The flip side of avoiding last minute cramming into the morning's wee hours is keeping up with assignments daily, a process Steven took seriously. Before engaging in playing any video games, he completed his homework, again, not an earth-shattering breakthrough approach, just a matter of establishing a positive habit.

What impressed me about Steven's commitment to earning straight A's was a mindset shift involving a new label. He thought of himself as an A student. 4.0, became more than a goal. It was his identity.

I thought about it and agree that positive labels pack a powerful punch. Adopting a new persona was a theory worth testing, and I did. After contemplating where to start, I purchased a new workout shirt that reads: #Fierce. It is pink (yeah, I'm such a girly-girl) and cute and something new to wear to the gym, a place I dread. Staying away from my workout schedule is not an option because "The Punisher," my personal trainer (actually his name is Brad) expects me to show up. But here's the thing, I now have a new label. When I brand myself #Fierce, I act the part performing more like an individual who enjoys pumping iron and strength training than a sleep-deprived class C student who can barely make it through the last set of chest flies.

Want to change the way life is grading you? Change your label. You can over-perform in school, at work, or on the playing field. Begin by instituting some positive habits, and be sure to create a winning new identity.

# Breaking My Golden Rule

I HUNG UP THE PHONE, breathed a sigh of relief, and took stock of my emotions. The call I just completed carried me far out of my comfort zone. The action I took was uncharacteristic, and yet I felt no remorse, or more importantly, no guilt.

Like many individuals, women, in particular, I fall into the tribe of people pleasers. Recently a committee placed me in a volunteer position without my consent. My downfall was, after much deliberation (which should have been a red flag, as a coach I'm trained to know better), I said yes. So what's the problem? I guess you can call it integrity, once I give my word, it's golden. I never go back on it. Indeed an honorable characteristic, but there have been several instances when sticking to my guns, caused significant stress, as was the case with this volunteer position.

What do you do when you've made the wrong decision, and your self-imposed moral code stands firm against turning back? My answer was first to phone a friend. I called upon someone with excellent judgment who reviewed the situation objectively, with no agenda. After presenting the facts, my friend Barb provided wise and rational feedback. She advised I ask that someone else take over. Hmm, my brain translated quit. Ouch, that meant going against my golden rule. I thanked her and decided to sleep on it.

One of the lessons I've learned over the years is not to act irrationally. Postpone a decision, if possible. Research suggests getting a good night's sleep is beneficial for multiple reasons. During rest, the brain clears itself of toxins then actively seeks other situations helpful in resolving the problem. This rang true for me.

The next morning I reviewed a past situation when I stubbornly refused to reverse a "Yes, I'll do it," even though I had ample time to do so. As I recalled sucking it up and honoring that commitment for an entire year, my decision became crystal clear. Taking the moral high ground is indeed an admirable trait, but in reality, this wasn't a level playing field. I did not volunteer; the team railroaded me into this position.

Sometimes no is the right answer. If you've made the wrong decision and it will harm no one to reverse it, do so. Living with yes, and secretly resenting it, is unproductive and unhealthy. There is always a lesson to absorb. I realized the better choice was to ignore the peer pressure and gracefully say no when asked.

# Playing Your Hunch

A FEW WEEKS AGO, I attended a speech contest. One of the contestants gave a very humorous talk about surviving a harrowing adventure while on vacation. What he thought would be an exciting escapade evolved into a giant scam. Our hero admitted his naiveté in ignoring the many red flags he experienced early on. He titled his speech, "Beware of Red Flags," as a lesson for the audience.

We all know what those red flags are. We've felt them. It's that queasy, uneasy feeling signaling our brain something is not quite right. When those crimson warnings arise, the most prudent thing to do is heed them. Often we ignore these caution signals and forge full steam ahead. As was the speaker's case, the man was just too pumped up to stop and think, eventually finding himself in a heap of trouble. The result was a hefty hit to his bank account.

Red flags pop up in a myriad of life experiences. Take the dating scene, for example. Remember that guy you started seeing last year? Your best friend warned you something was amiss, your mom was not a member of his fan club, and in the end, you wasted six months on a relationship journey to nowhere. Or what about that "win-win" financial investment your cousin said was a sure thing? You probably knew it was a long shot, but wanting a quick windfall so desperately, you took an unsafe risk, and it cost you, big time.

Avoid tripping over red flags by tapping into your intuition and observing what your body is trying to tell you. The phrase "gut reaction" is an accurate description of a distress warning exhibited physically. Experiencing a sour or churning stomach when faced with a decision is the internal red flag cautioning danger.

We are all blessed with intuition. Even Bill Gates, who is no doubt surrounded by highly paid talented advisors, admits, "Often you have to rely on intuition." Individuals who are successful in developing this internal insight do make better decisions.

Try it out this week. Place a moratorium on making snap decisions and pay attention to early warning signals. Tune in to the wisdom of your psyche and physical reactions as you consider which path to take. View a hunch as not just a fleeting thought but a valuable piece of information. After considerable reflection, see if you can clear the field of those red flags and feel more confident about your decision; if not, you know what to do. Just walk away.

# Pushing of the Broom

A FEW YEARS AGO, I met a man named Michael, who told me how much he looked forward to owning a push broom. No, he wasn't in the custodial services industry; my new acquaintance was an artistic director at a rented local playhouse.

Each season, when the final curtain goes down, Michael takes up the broom and gives the stage a thorough once over. Pushing it across the floor inspires and reminds him to keep pursuing his dream of one day possessing his own 250-seat theater, equipped with a broom.

Giant-sized dreams are passion-based. Oprah believes: "Passion is energy. Feel the power that comes from focusing on what excites you." Michael of the push broom dream did not start his career as an artistic director, but he was always passionate about theater. Like many individuals in the entertainment industry, his theatrical career began in the chorus line. Over the years, he honed his skills, added significant credits to his acting career, and subsequently evolved into his role as the executive of a theatrical organization.

Many aspiring entrepreneurs have the push broom dream. It begins with defining a career that makes your heart sing. Passion is the foundation upon which creative ideas flourish and grow.

It's the driving force fueling your dreams and keeping you going when life socks you with setbacks, drowns you in disappointments, and erects speed bumps in your path. Passion brings out the incurable optimist in you and provides the energy and stamina required to achieve your goals and become the best version of yourself.

Are you not feeling the passion yet? Granted, it is not always evident. Sometimes it lingers beneath the surface, requiring some excavation. Often clients approach me with a desire to reinvent themselves but have no idea where to begin. One recommendation is to visit a bookstore. Of the many departments, where do you linger? For me, it's easy. I could spend an entire day in self-help racks. It was during this very exercise I discovered a passion for coaching.

Another approach is to follow your curiosity. I love the scenes in the movie "Julie and Julia" when a determined Julia Child embarks upon several endeavors before experiencing the defining moment when she discovered food was her true passion. So, sign up for courses that interest you, interview individuals in a profession you would like to know more about, keep searching, and keep an open mind. Eventually, you will uncover your passion.

A word of warning, once you announce to the world and begin to follow your dream, you may get push-back. Perhaps your parents want you to take another career path, or your spouse balks at you taking a step back to get two steps forward. Remember, it's your dream, and you get to write your own story. Stay committed, persevere, and set your sights on acquiring a push broom of your own.

# My Favorite Four Letter Word

WHILE SORTING THE MAIL, I locked in on the four-letter word spanning about a quarter of the magazine cover. There in print was one of my favorite words - GRIT. Along with Angela Duckworth, the nation's self-proclaimed cheerleader of grit, I believe that the power-packed factor is a strong contender for the number one trait of successful people.

Since Angela and I are members of the same philosophical tribe, I immediately stopped sorting the mail and read the article promoting her 2016 best-seller book, *Grit: The Power of Passion and Perseverance*. Next, I watched her TED Talk, then toggled over to her website and took the Grit Scale test.

Why am I so over-the-top about the grit theme? For starters, let's use Angela as an example. During her childhood, her father often complained about her intellectual limitations. Turns out decades later, Angela was awarded a "genius grant" from the MacArthur Foundation for her work on the role grit plays in educational achievement. Here's the kicker, her research defines grit as an accurate predictor of both classroom and workplace success.

In her TED talk, Angela commented that some of her most successful students did not have "stratospheric IQ scores." As a researcher, she found that one characteristic emerged as a significant predictor of success. It was grit, which Angela defines as "passion and perseverance for very long-term goals."

The data boils down to this. Success isn't dependent on good looks, family income, or talent. Gritty means slugging it out day after day to pursue your goals, staying motivated, and not giving up until you reach the finish line. Just writing that sentence makes me want to do my happy dance and fist pump with joy.

My message today, is, any child in school and any adult in the workplace can make it. So parents, teach your children to be gritty. It's a work ethic; role model it for them, show them you never give up.

Careerists, young and old, what may have impeded success in the past need not predict the future. Be sure to check out Angela's Grit Scale and see how you score: https://angeladuckworth.com/grit-scale/ Make the needed corrections, and if you need more inspiration, read her book.

Will accomplishing your goal be easy now that you have the secret sauce? Of course not, but here's an anonymous quote I found to give you that extra needed push, "It's gonna get harder before it gets easier. It will get better. You just gotta make it through the hard stuff first."

Yep, it won't be a cakewalk, but you can nail it if you employ that four-letter word.

# Gut Reaction Whispers

EVER GO THROUGH WITH SOMETHING knowing it won't end well? That happened to me recently. To my credit, I tried to gracefully get out of doing a business transaction with someone who did not have my complete trust. Perhaps I was too polite, or maybe I was allowing this individual to gain my confidence. The bottom line, I ignored the red flags and forged ahead.

The warning sign I neglected to heed was intuition. We are all gifted with that potent tool helping us navigate through life's crossroads. Some call it a little voice; others identify it as that queasy feeling something is amiss, but we all experience a gut reaction whispering the signals. According to the experts at "Psychology Today," intuition is the brain on autopilot, performing actions of processing information without our conscious awareness. Scientific data supports the "trust your gut" philosophy. Our brain and gut connect by an extensive network of neurons and a composition of chemicals and hormones. This information superhighway has been named the brain-gut axis. It serves to provide input.

Here's an example. In hindsight, I realize the exact point where my intuition kicked in. During my first conversation with this individual, my brain was processing unconscious clues. Red flags went down on the field as I listened to her voice and studied her facial expressions. At that point, I suspected she might be a bad actor playing a part, so I made an effort to say no. She continued to pressure me, and unfortunately, I waffled and allowed her to convince me otherwise. It's somewhat ironic my lesson learned here is trusting your gut, which is the advice I often dole out to others.

What are some ways we can live more intuitively? Begin by becoming fully aware of that intuitive hit, then engage your rational mind to sort out what action to take. Doing so saved me a serious injury once. Driving down a busy California freeway one day, I noticed a truck several car lengths ahead of me transporting a picnic table in his vehicle. Something told me I was in danger. Within seconds, the picnic table flew from the truck, almost smashing into my car. Had I not been aware of imminent danger, my car would have been struck. But sensing this, I quickly changed lanes. In this situation, my intuition was on high alert. Other warning signals are chills, pain in the gut or chest, or the sudden onset of a headache.

Yes, I understand it's not always easy. We've all heard stories of a bride or groom left at the altar. Hurt and embarrassment are tough ways to end a relationship, but better than making a colossal mistake.

So, listen up. Know that you have a voice within that doesn't use words. Pay attention to that silent angel and, when possible, add that data as a tool to enhance definite conclusions. By doing so, you will make safer, wiser decisions.

# Upstaging Success

OVER BRUNCH, MY FRIEND CATHY related a story about her days as a young waitress in Los Angeles. One morning during her shift, a hopeful starving-actor entered the restaurant asking for the least expensive nutritious item on the menu. Cathy provided advice and served him.

Upon completing his meal, the fellow realized he could not cover the full amount of the tab. My friend waved it off, saying she would make up any shortage for him, but the fellow insisted on making up the difference, and he did. For the next 30 minutes during a hectic business surge, he happily bussed all of the tables in her section.

After hearing Cathy's narrative, my friends and I broke out in smiles and nodded in agreement. Whether it's getting the last squeeze out of a flattened tube of toothpaste or stretching your meal budget, if you're creative about employing some techniques, you can always accomplish your goal.

It's worth noting our young actor friend used a few key strategies. First, he asked for menu advice. In response, Cathy pointed out an inexpensive entrée. When you need something as simple as a menu suggestion, or on the flip side, valuable career advice, do not be reticent in getting help. Too often, fear gets in the way of asking for assistance in getting to the next level. Remember that when you need a boost, or helping hand. Rather than tough it out alone, speak up.

The young man's goal was getting hired, but he knew to ace the upcoming audition he required sustenance. Like our wannabe star, you must acquire the tools needed to get to the goal line. You'll never reach your destination on an empty tank, or get that promotion without the requisite skills. Plan ahead, and then do the work.

Lastly, and what I admired most about our hero, he dealt with the bumps in the road. We all know there is no such thing as a smooth, safe path to achieving an ambitious goal. When you're trying to move your career forward or declutter and remodel your home, don't get discouraged with a setback, deal with it. Perhaps the actor thought ahead about how he'd address a financial shortage, or maybe it was just a quick reaction. Whatever the case, he found a viable way to resolve the situation.

One final thought. Life is messy. For those of you with perfectionist tendencies, listen up. The best-laid plans are subject to unexpected chaos. Hang on tight when you ride that bumpy rail, get creative and stay flexible as you maneuver your way to success.

# Partnering with Dummies

IT WAS A MAGICAL EVENING. After dinner, we walked over to The Mirage to see comedian, ventriloquist, and celebrity impressionist Terry Fator. Upon our arrival, a hostess informed me the six of us would be seated in second-row center and not the seats we originally purchased. Shocked, I realized this was a purely random happening as no one in my party held any kind of status. A surprise offering like this happened to me once before when American Airlines asked me if I would mind sitting in first class. Who was I to question how the gods of unexpected free upgrades select their targets? Giving the usher my most gracious smile while my husband attended to a gratuity, our happy party strutted to our VIP seats.

Before long, I was so mesmerized with the performance I forgot Fator, (who, according to Wikipedia, can create over 100 impressions), was the voice behind the entire show. It wasn't until much later I thought about how many hours this ace ventriloquist logged honing his craft and played backstage at local state fairs before he finally hit the big time. Seeing the show from second-row center may have been lucky for me, but Fator's command of the spotlight had little to do with luck.

I was curious about Terry's life before he was catapulted to success when named the million-dollar winner of *American's Got Talent*. My research revealed a winning combination of three factors I've dubbed Fator Factors.

Before his initial gig at a church picnic, Fator learned the art of ventriloquism meant practice, practice, practice.

Fator Factor Number One: Discipline. No doubt, when the other kids headed to the park with gloves, balls, and bats, Terry remained home in front of his mirror with the Willie Talk dummy he purchased from Sears.

Fator Factor Number Two: Resilience. Years of performing at small venues with low exposure meant exercising his resilience muscle. Terry admits the lowest part of his career was playing at a 1,000-seat theatre with a paid audience of one. Hitting rock bottom means getting back up for another round armed with resilience.

Fator Factor Number Three: Support. When Terry hit his late thirties, he almost quit. It was his family who encouraged him to keep going.

Take a moment to re-read and digest the Fator Factors. It's going to take grit and guts, but if you are determined to achieve your dream, you will. Stay disciplined and practice resilience. Regarding number three, you may not have a supportive family, but I guarantee you have people in your life that will cheer you on. Share your goal with those who are a positive influence on you. When the chips are down, they will build you back up. You're no dummy. You can do this!

# Success

In Summary:

* Say no when you should
* Brand yourself appropriately
* Create a winning identity
* Heed your intuition
* Increase your grit level
* Discipline yourself
* Interact with your support team
* Watch for red flags
* Uncover your passion
* Write your own story
* Get creative
* Stay flexible

# Goal Management
# Keeping Score

"Vision without action is a daydream.
Action without vision is a nightmare. "

— JAPANESE PROVERB

# I Was a Nora

OPTIMISM RUNS HIGH IN JANUARY. Most of us get pumped up about several challenges like creating a fitness routine, losing weight, expanding our business, or earning that coveted promotion. Typically somewhere around the middle of March upon reviewing our goal list, it's not unusual to see we are severely off-track. What went wrong? My hypothesis is; we tend to bite off too much too soon.

For example, my friend Nora created a list of her top ten goals. On January 1st, she tried to leap from a non-existent exercise routine to a five day, 5:00 a.m. gym regimen while juggling her daily responsibilities and working on nine other goals. I called her today to see how she was progressing. Nora admitted as hard as she tried, she could not keep up the pace. Her gym visits dwindled, and she confessed to little or no progress with her remaining goals.

We often set ourselves up for failure by overcompensating our lack of achievement in previous years. The new system we create for ourselves unravels, and we become discouraged. More than one client has walked in my office, lamenting the inability to get to the goal line. If this sounds familiar, don't despair, but do read on.

Years ago, I was a Nora. While popping the cork on a great bottle of the bubbly each New Year's Eve, visions of tremendous success scenarios swirled around in my head. I watched joyfully as the ball dropped, kissed my husband, and claimed the New Year as my time to soar. It didn't take long to see those visions break like the bubbles in a glass of champagne. My epiphany came when I read Gretchen Rubin's book *The Happiness Project*. What fascinated me was Gretchen's thirty-day concept. Gretchen spent an entire month focused on a limited number of goals. I found pairing my list down to only one goal each month works.

Want to avoid the mid-March blues or any angst over goals that have flat-lined? Create a list of no more than twelve annual goals. Decide where you will start. This year I want to streamline my life, reduce clutter, and finish every project I start. My January activity involves ridding myself of ten things every day. They can be physical items or time-wasting activities that crowd my calendar. Give it a try. One month, one goal. Stay the course, and on December 31st, your goal scorecard will reveal completed items. Now break out the champagne!

# Clearing the Bar
# Big Time

RECENTLY, A FRIEND WHILE COMPLIMENTING me on my business's name, "Raise the Bar High," asked how I selected it. Good question. I explained I am a country-western fan. One day I heard a song by Sugarland with the lyric "tired of shooting too low, so raise the bar high," and I thought that's it! (The song, written by Jennifer Nettles, Kristian Bush, and Tim Owens reached the top of the Billboard Hot Country Songs chart.) It was the perfect name because I enjoy coaching people with lofty goals who are ready to do the work.

Think about it. What do you get when you set a goal reached with minimal effort? No doubt the answer is, you receive the minimum return. So don't cheat yourself by low-level goals. Set a huge goal, and you may surprise yourself by finding you have more potential than you thought.

Super-sized goals require both dedicated focus and a commitment to stay in the game. In my mind, one ingredient to the secret sauce of a stick-to-it mentality involves fun. That's right. I'm talking about celebrating. After all, who doesn't love a celebration? It helps us truly enjoy the journey.

Try this short exercise. Go to the drawing board. Sketch out a massive goal and break it down into steps. Next, decide where the milestones fall. For example, we can all relate to weight loss goals. Let's go with 50 pounds as a number. Setting our benchmarks in 10-pound increments makes sense. We can stop for a beat and savor the victory with a small reward. (Of course, celebrating with a non-food item is recommended). Recognizing how far we've come is highly motivational--acknowledging the specific milestone drives us on toward the finish line.

Here's another hint to attaining broad goals. Practice the power of patience. Acknowledge that nothing happens overnight. A child, who wants to win a spelling bee, drills, right? If you're going to run a marathon, you need to train, correct? Build that mentality into your daily thought process. Tell yourself your mountain is not too big to climb; it just requires patience and a steady effort.

So dream big, visualize yourself raising the bar high and clearing it. You may not jump high enough on the first run, but don't let that deter you. Get right back up and try again. You will get there!

Ready to tackle the week and work on your BIGGEST goals? Excellent. Stop reading and start Now!

# Show Up, Lace Up, Warm Up, and Go!

WITH A HEAVY SIGH, MY client took a seat in the office, complaining about the multiple projects needing attention and his lack of motivation to tackle even one. I nodded, as it was not unusual in my practice to have clients voice that particular frustration. Yes, we all go through periods of diminished energy and experience feelings of not being up to the challenge. Long ago, I learned a partial remedy for combating inertia is, as Woody Allen so aptly expressed it, "just showing up."

The fact that the young man arrived on time for his scheduled coaching session was indeed a start. Reminding him of this fact, I also shared the story of a baseball player who developed a system to pull himself out of a lethargic funk and ready both mind and body for a win. This pitcher created a routine that consisted of jogging back and forth on the field, stretching hips and hamstrings, throwing some light warm-up pitches from the mound, and then heading back to the dugout. He diligently performed these sequenced movements before every game. The routine not only succeeded in getting his body warmed up, but it also coaxed out a positive attitude resulting in his pre-game winning mentality.

Most of us don't bound out of bed with the enthusiasm of a four-year-old ready for a day at the beach. Our minds and bodies often need a little prodding to get the message there is work to be done. As adults, establishing a rhythmic series of steps, inspires action. A friend of mine jumps out of bed and into her running shoes, convincing her feet they are heading to the gym sooner or later. When arriving at my desk each morning, I go through an orchestrated dance, with a strong cup of coffee in hand. Rather than immediately diving into a complex project, I warm up by reviewing my schedule, reading an inspirational blog or two, and then knocking-off some mundane administrative tasks. The process takes about twenty minutes, and by that time, I am alert and ready to take on the day.

Some may dispute the utter simplicity of showing up and going through the motions. But just as a ballerina warms up at the barre with a series of plies and Ronds de Jambe before taking the floor, or a chef preps food before creating a gourmet entrée, we all need a little windup routine before we can knock one out of the ballpark.

# To Get it Right – Write

WHILE PEEKING IN MY HUSBAND'S office, I observed him humming while assembling his new desk chair. Upon giving the scene a second glance, I noticed, contrary to the male stereotype, he was reading the directions! It reminded me of a study I read. Research from the University of Tromso in Norway found men were faster at assembling flat-pack furniture than women. IKEA did their own study and reported men constructed furniture more quickly than women even when they didn't read the manual.

Well, study or no study, after many false starts, I've learned to opt for a roadmap. Following a whim and taking an unchartered course doesn't work for me. Why? Because most of the time, "winging it", rarely gets me a successful landing.

If you want to be successful, you need a plan. The first commandment of creating a plan is it must be in writing. You don't have to trust me on this. Scientific data backs up that rule. Psychology professor Dr. Gail Matthews, who studied the subject for over 30 years, found committing your goals to paper can increase your possibility of success by 40%--convinced yet?

Now that you are ready to commit your plan to writing you can create your goal map online or in a notebook. Or, another alternative is to buy one off the shelf. As a career coach, I often review products designed to keep us on track. A few years ago, my acquisition was the "Full Focus Planner," created to keep annual goals visible by integrating a productivity methodology into monthly, weekly, and daily commitments. This year I am seriously entrenched in learning the system of bullet journaling.

My preference is a written system because (don't laugh, wait, okay go ahead and have a good chuckle if you wish) I still think of paper as a technology. Want another paper-oriented method? Do some research on mind mapping. Created as a graphic tool, this technique unlocks brain potential. All you need to produce a goal mind map is blank paper, colored pencils, and a quiet corner where you can tap into your imagination and chart your course.

If you prefer doing the work online, many platforms are available. A quick Google search will keep you busy for hours, determining which resource would work best for you. Some templates are even free. It doesn't matter if you purchase a system or create your own. Utilize whatever methodology suits your style. The bottom line is that written goals provide clarity, focus, and direction.

Opting out of an instructional road map might get the furniture built, but it is doubtful you will complete your goals without direction. As Yogi Berra so aptly put it, "If you don't know where you are going, you may end up somewhere else."

# A Wise Investment

WHILE CONCLUDING A RECENT PHONE call, I experienced a warm and fuzzy feeling. I just completed a resume for a new client. Before we hung up, she expressed joy and appreciation for the document showcasing her skills. Naturally, delighting a client with a work product is the objective, but way down deep; I knew my happiness was more about her. Although I am unaware of the back-story, I sensed she had fallen on some hard times. She told me she promised herself to start investing in numero uno and kicked it off with an updated professional resume.

Do you have a vision of what you want to accomplish this year? Allocating your time and money is one of the essential tasks in creating a happy and successful life. Perhaps one of your goals this year is to save for a new home or a trip to Maui. If so, bravo! I applaud you. But before you squirrel away all your money for the new digs or a plane ticket, what part of your earnings have you earmarked for your personal development? Make that a priority when budgeting each year.

If you want to pump up your resume, have you considered returning to school? Enrolling in coursework to upgrade your knowledge base can not only improve your resume and potential future earnings, but it can also ignite a new passion and set you on a path to further success. Adding to your skill base bolsters your self-confidence as you continue learning and growing.

If you're shaking your head bemoaning lack of funds for college tuition, don't be discouraged. Learning a new skill can be accomplished by investing little more than your time. By doing a Google search, you'll find many inexpensive courses, seminars, and online-based training. You can learn a language, improve your public speaking skills, or tackle a time management course to improve your efficiency.

Self-development also encompasses your well-being. So if you are a retiree, these words also apply to you. Have you set any goals this year to learn a new hobby or improve your physical well-being? If not, get started. You can join a gym or find a cost-free way to exercise. You-Tube is an excellent resource for learning how to play the piano or create an English garden. The significant investment is time. How will you allocate it?

Dale Carnegie, a man born on a poor Missouri farm, later became an author and founder of a successful training company. Consider this quote from Mr. Carnegie: "If you are not in the process of becoming the person you want to be, you are automatically engaged in becoming the person you don't want to be." Wise words from a, wise man. I love that guy!

# Success Strategies From the Bleachers

WHEN I HEARD MY CLIENT say he was going for a shut-out, I did a mental cheer. Not only did he declare a firm commitment, but he also used a metaphor that delighted me as I immediately thought of baseball. Pitching a shut-out means one pitcher goes the entire nine innings without giving up a run. My client, a winning business owner, was ready to go the distance and wipe out the competition, and I knew he could.

I have a strong affection for America's favorite pastime, as baseball offers so many life lessons. If you want an education on what it takes to be successful in business or life, consider these game strategies:

**Step up to the plate:** Ever watch a player who is "on deck?" He is the guy next in line to bat. Observe him vigorously warming up his arms by swinging a weighted bat. Then, in turn, he takes his place at the plate, ready to move the game forward by making contact with the ball.

So, getting in the game begins with preparing in the on-deck circle before stepping up to the plate. Set a goal, then, take action by connecting and moving forward with your plan.

**Stealing:** Although stealing is legal only in baseball, a steal's very nature is fraught with risk. To execute a steal successfully, a runner must have perfect timing and instincts. Ready to take that calculated risk? If you feel the time is right, go for it. Sure, you might get tagged out, but you won't know unless you try.

**Sacrifice bunt:** In this play, the batter, who is typically sacrificed, bunts the ball to advance another player on base. Being a reliable team player means giving up some personal glory for the greater good of the team.

**Change up pitch:** This off-speed pitch is thrown to look like a fastball. It surprises the batter by arriving slower at the plate. The operative word here is change. Learn to anticipate change. If a change-up or a curveball situation takes you by surprise, deal with it.

**Covering all the bases:** An infielder's job is to stand close to the base, waiting to force a runner out when the ball is in play. Protect your career by building a safety net. Have an updated resume and continually network to make connections should a business downturn impact you. Regarding any critical life event, cover your bases by having a backup plan.

**Out of the ballpark:** Happy is the player who steps to the plate and slugs a home run.

Perhaps you're not a baseball fan, but you must admit there is a substantial similarity between these metaphors and creating a successful life. Former major league pitcher, coach and manager Tommy Lasorda quipped, "There are three types of baseball players: Those you make it happen, those who watch it happen, and those who wonder what happens." Be the one who makes it happen by putting these baseball strategies into practice, and you'll soon be belting one out of the park.

# Goal Management

In Summary:

- Invest in yourself
- Super-size your goals
- Practice patience
- Employ the 30-day concept
- Just show up
- Create a warm-up
- Take a calculated risk
- Anticipate change
- Design a road map
- Write out goals

# Time Management
# Tasks and Time

"The bad news is time flies. The good
news is, you're the pilot"

— MICHAEL ALTSHULER

# Hit The Breaker Box

THE OTHER DAY I RECEIVED a note from my friend Jenny. She read my column about turning down the noise and had this to say: "I try to remind myself every day to make quiet time for myself. I'm getting better at it. I remember when we lost power for most of the evening and into the early morning during a bad storm. After the storm was over, my husband and I (and our little dog) went for a walk holding hands and enjoying the moments; then we came home, got out the candles, sat on the couch and talked about life. We laughed and talked for hours. It was so enjoyable, no TV, no computer, or Internet thanks to no power. Now I sometimes think about hitting the breaker box to get my husband away from the TV. Also, to divert my attention from the computer."

Messing with the breaker box might be a bit on the drastic side, but my friend has the right idea. Unplugging from the outside world can be challenging, but as evidenced by Jenny's story, when we let go of the need for continual online linkage, we create more room in our lives for people who matter. Sure your 500+ friends on Facebook and connections on Instagram, LinkedIn, and Twitter are real people, but nothing is more important than sharing one-on-one time with those you love.

There are other advantages in powering-down all electronic devices and experiencing the world without all the static. Ceasing to consume the myriad of information bombarding us daily through the Internet and media gives us time to process and create. Writing fresh content for my columns or blog doesn't happen by surfing the net or reading posts on Facebook. I need quiet think-time to design a meaningful message that creates value for my readers.

Ever stopped to consider the addictive nature of constantly tuning-in? A friend of mine lets the world know where she is at all times by using the "check-in" feature on Facebook. She is one of my favorite people, but I don't have to know when and where she gets her pedicures.

Ready to schedule a timeout? Try designating one day a week to unplug. If you cannot manage an entire day, try four hours. Take time to embrace silence, enjoy nature, or connect with a loved one to experience some hand-holding and romantic walks. If all else fails, turn off your phone, light the candles, and hit the breaker box!

# Another Four-Letter Word

IT WAS AN EVENTFUL WEEK. A close friend welcomed a new baby girl into the family while another loved one said a final good-bye to her mother. What both events had in common was a period of waiting. Joyful anticipation built over the months as the new mom and her extended family prepared for the birth of a child, but if you've ever lost a severely ill aging parent, you feel the pain of the wait as those precious minutes slip away.

There are all kinds of waiting periods in life. Waiting to meet your soul mate, waiting for a house to sell, waiting for a latte at Starbucks, waiting for summer to begin, and the list goes on and on.

In the past, I sucked at waiting, continually wishing I could fast-forward time. Perhaps, that is a common ailment in our "I want it now," world. True, some things are out of my control, and waiting periods fall into that category. Over the years, I've learned to utilize the wait time wisely and respect the process.

Whoever coined the phrase, "Good things come to those who wait," had a point. For example, a few years ago, one of my single clients (let's call her Tami) was obsessed with finding a mate.

She kept replaying "What's wrong with me" scenarios. Tami is a beautiful, hardworking accountant, but spending most of her waking hours at the office took a toll on her ability to converse about anything other than balance sheets and journal entries.

My suggestion involved reducing her working hours, making room for a hobby. Consequently, Tami enrolled in several gourmet cooking classes and even began blogging about vegetarian cuisine. By busying herself with a hobby and back-burnering her focus on waiting for "the one" to show up, she started feeling fulfilled outside of the office. Oh, and did I mention Mr. Wonderful eventually surfaced? It turns out she married the chef instructor of her Pasta 101 course.

Tami's experience is indicative of periods that require we patiently go into a holding pattern. So how should you deal with a life event you are hoping to hurry along? First, accept that "wait" is not a nasty four-letter word. Change your focus and make some plans while you're sitting it out. By doing so, in the interim, you might find you're having the time of your life.

# Hanging with Arnie

ARNIE RUSHED INTO MY OFFICE, suit jacket flapping behind him. He sat down, delivered a heavy sigh, and complained of over-scheduling. I giggled, reminding him that he was retired. In my mind, his calendar overload was self-inflicted. A serious look crossed his face as he shrugged his shoulders and checked an alert from his phone. Rolling his eyes, he muttered something about a golf game.

Getting down to business, I soon understood Arnie's problem. He developed a habit of accepting every social invitation that came along. Although this might not sound like much of a problem, it can lead to a dysfunctional lifestyle. It is sometimes dubbed the "can't say no syndrome." I have coached many individuals who fall into this category.

Delving deeper into why the "no" word was missing from Arnie's vocabulary, he admitted there were many times he would rather stay home with Chinese takeout and a good book. He participated whenever he got invited to an event because he did not want to offend anyone. I pushed back, asserting there are multiple polite ways to decline an invitation. It seemed to me there was more to this than a case of overly polite manners. After more discussion, it became evident Arnie's real issue surrounded the "left behind syndrome."

His reason for going along with the crowd is not as trite as it sounds. Social media has penetrated our lives. Sitting home alone, observing the partying gang's posting on social media can elicit feelings of being left out, but only if you let it.

Whether you are a baby boomer, Gen X, Millennial, or Gen Y hanging out with yourself should be a satisfying and enjoyable experience. Carving out time from your schedule to spend developing your creative side, going for a solitary run, or sitting in silence and quieting your mind is a healthy choice. Solitude does not equate to loneliness. Developing a deep connection with yourself leads to clarity on life choices and future goals.

About a week later, Arnie returned to my office proudly announcing he canceled a social engagement, turned off his smartphone, and spent an afternoon alone puttering in the garage with his playlist softly streaming in the background. When I inquired how he felt about not going out, Arnie flashed a grin admitting he felt relieved. He chose to do what made him happy and realized he wasn't bored or feeling left out. He declared, "I'm a rather cool guy to hang out with." Agreed! Hanging with Arnie is fun.

# The Four-Legged Stool

SOME MONTHS AGO, I AWOKE at 3:00 am and, in fits of micro-terror, began experiencing the "Lion's Syndrome." What's that? It's a label explaining the emotion we experience when feeling overwhelmed by overload. Maura Thomas, an accomplished productivity guru and the author of *Personal Productivity Secrets*, describes the syndrome as being, "Based on an anecdote about an animal tamer's method of subduing a lion by presenting multiple "threats" (four legs of a stool) simultaneously. The lion gets confused and retreats from the chaos." Simply put, lions, like people, get overwhelmed when trying to focus on too many things at once.

You can relate, right? You feel helpless like you're drowning in enormous waves of tasks crashing down around you. According to Ms. Thomas, the answer to overcoming Lion's Syndrome is achieving a state of flow and engaging in optimal performance. Yes, I hear you muttering something like easier said than done efficiency expert lady. Well, stay with me a moment. She didn't get to be a TEDx speaker and regular contributor to the Harvard Business Review by accident.

In her TEDx talk, Maura shares, "No amount of time management will ever change the number of demands on our attention." She suggests we forget time management, calling it an outdated concept. Sounds radical, right?

So how do we replace the concept of time management? Her recommendation is turning our thoughts to "attention management." Master your attention and avoid Lion's Syndrome. You can benefit from watching her TEDx Talk, entitled, "Control Your Attention, Control Your Life!" in which she makes a very simple, but profound statement. "How you spend your time is only relevant to the extent of how you also devote your attention."

Increased productivity involves taking control of your attention and becoming vigilant of time stealers. It might take a little practice, but get focused on stopping anyone or anything, trying to divert your attention from a task.

Your challenge this week is to stop the sabotage. Identify the items and activities that rob you of laser-sharp focus. Some are easily defined, like stop checking your email every five minutes and start sending your calls to voice mail. Others may be more obscure. Forget trying to multi-task, you know there is no such thing, it's just a lie we tell ourselves. Once you get good at this, you can find your flow and engage your creative genius in meaningful output. Even better, you can sleep blissfully through the night rather than waking up in a cold sweat at 3:00 am.

# Crush The Time Killers

MY CLIENT WALKED INTO MY office wearing a long face and tossing off a lackluster greeting. Noticing the gloomy aura, I inquired about the cause. Morgan complained of a recent lack of productivity. Her entire week was fraught with stops and starts, tons of interruptions, project stalls, and no substantive progress. I could relate. We've all had those upside-down unproductive days that sometimes last a week. But we are not doing it right if each day ends in frustration.

Getting back on track requires some introspection, followed by operational changes. Morgan is helpful and accommodating. Although that is an admirable quality, acting as the go-to guru gal who frequently stops to help the rest of the team, means she must set some limits. Around the clock, availability is an invitation for others to interrupt, taking focus away from the task. If, like Morgan, you find yourself in that position, change that dynamic by firmly signaling you are in the middle of an important project and must stay focused.

Another factor in riding the express train to productivity is timing. Our internal clock plays a significant role in how much we accomplish during a given day. Be aware of peak times. Research proves creating momentum in the early hours of the day offers a psychological boost. If morning is when your engine runs at peak performance, schedule the heavy lifting activities for that time of day. A work process also counts. Experts recommend, powering through a 90-minute segment, then taking a ten-minute break to refresh.

Flex your delegation muscles whenever it is prudent and possible. During my session with Morgan, we discovered she processed work that could be handed off to her staff. Simply put, either at work or home, if you can delegate a task to someone else, do it. Don't be too proud to ask for help. When feeling stressed and overwhelmed, look around. Zero-in on a set of helping hands and stop trying to go it alone.

Meetings can be a giant time killer. Sure, many are mandatory, but not all. I suggested that my client review her schedule for the upcoming week and decide what meetings could be shortened or eliminated. When involved in mandatory meetings, assign a timekeeper and a facilitator to keep all participants focused on the agenda.

If you're consistently planted behind your desk, you're doing it wrong. Sprinkle five-minute "walkabouts" throughout your day. Not only does this get your blood pumping, but also your thoughts receive a mini vacation. Scientific studies report that brief mental breaks help you stay focused.

At our next session, Morgan reported that she aced her work-week by employing the productivity strategies we reviewed. Small changes can lead to big success. Give it a try. Power through the week, and you'll have reason to celebrate on the weekend.

# 60 Minutes is No Big Deal, Or is It?

EACH YEAR, AS THE END of daylight savings time approaches, I feel like doing a happy dance. The idea of turning back the clock is so appealing. Since most of us are always racing against time, being gifted with an extra hour to do anything our heart desires is pure bliss. Over the years, I've found creative ways to enjoy those additional 60 minutes, leaving me with an extra boost of fulfillment.

This year I blew it! I ended up doing nothing but staying in bed, practicing laziness. I could excuse myself if I were exhausted and needed the extra snooze time, but on the contrary, I found myself eyes-wide-open awake. Finally, I called myself out and trudged out of bed, feeling defeated. I had no one to blame but myself.

How did it happen that I failed to utilize the hour to accomplish a task or even joyfully and mindfully soak in the quiet of daybreak? As a time management student, I can tell you in three words where I messed up, failure to plan. When you are not intentional with time and energy, nothing happens. My favorite Chinese proverb illustrates this fact: "Talk does not cook rice."

As a career coach, I spend countless hours helping clients get to the finish line by continual prodding with straightforward questions. "When will you do that?" is my constant refrain. This query prompts the individual to schedule the activity. Once an action gets firmly planted on the calendar, the success rate exponentially increases.

Designing a goal is easy, but it is essential to understand there is a price to be paid on the way to achievement. To accomplish our life dreams, we must be willing to pay the price in effort, action, sacrifice, and time. Whiling away one hour may seem like a minuscule incident, but in comparison, think of how much you can accomplish in an hour. The path to the goal line holds various bite-sized action items, many of which you can knock off in 60 minutes or less.

On that Sunday night, as I bade farewell to the day, I experienced a small heartbreak for not using that extra hour productively. Next year will not catch me in lethargic nothingness. When I sacrifice the hour as we spring ahead, I'll hatch a plan to recoup that time wisely. I've learned from Ben Franklin, who first conceived of daylight savings time in 1784 that "by failing to prepare, you are preparing to fail."

# Time Management

IN SUMMARY:

* Plan
* Prepare to wait
* Stay focused
* Eliminate time sucks
* Delegate
* Embrace me time
* Go offline
* Use your pause button
* Practice attention management

# Perfection
# Adjusting Your
# Standards

"The thing that is really hard, and really
amazing, is giving up on being perfect and
beginning the work of being yourself."

— ANNA QUINDLEN

# When is Enough Enough?

ONE OF MY FAVORITE CLIENTS came to me with a problem many of us share. In her quest for producing a stellar work product, Madison suffers from a dream-destroying syndrome. Any guess on what that is? I'll give you a hint. If you spend an inordinate amount of time tweaking a presentation, a working paper, or even a work of art, you know the problem is perfectionism. Yep, just another one of those "isms" we battle in our desire to have it all together.

Raising the bar high is a good thing. Sure I liked the phrase so much I gave my business that name. Setting high standards, striving for excellence, holding out for great, not good, again all excellent, but chasing perfectionism is an obsession. Spotting this fixation is easy. It happens when you find yourself agonizing over every little detail of whatever you're trying to accomplish. When you tweak and re-tweak, when your frown lines work over-time due to fretting, and the nasty naysayers in your head keep telling you it's not good enough, you have a problem.

Okay, now the good news. You are not hardwired with the perfection syndrome. No, you were not born that way. Once you realize that perfectionism is a fallacy, you can act on changing your thinking and curbing the obsession. Words matter! I suggest you omit the word perfect from your vocabulary.

Children get it. I once watched my six-year-old niece work on a school project involving a contest. Winners received a trip to the state capital. Alina quietly labored over the assignment for about forty minutes. Then with great fanfare, she pushed her chair away from her desk, stood up, and declared, "Good enough, that should get me to Lansing." With a broad smile, she headed out the door to have some fun. I don't know if she ever won the trip, but I know she was satisfied with her effort, and that was all that mattered.

So the next time you find yourself critically judging something you are working on, ask yourself one key question. Did you give it your best effort? If so, it's enough. You're done! Close up shop and move on. Find joy in the fact that you took the task seriously, you created a deliverable, and although it may, or may not, be award-winning, it's damn good. Then head out the door and have some fun.

# Lessons Learned on an Imaginary Flight

THE DREAM WAS SO ENLIGHTENING I wanted to linger in it for as long as possible. I stayed still without moving a muscle remaining connected to my dream state for another minute. When I finally turned to get out of bed, I made a solemn promise to retain the lesson provided by my nighttime experience.

My fascinating dream started in a panic. I was on a flight to Paris with a group of tourists, who were all strangers, when I realized I'd forgotten to bring any form of currency. Now in real life, that would be something I could resolve, but in this fantasy world, it meant spending two weeks in the City of Lights sans money for food, essentials, and souvenirs. I felt the pounding of a nasty stress headache. The thing I wanted at that moment, even more than money, was an Ibuprofen. Also, an item left behind.

Feeling utterly miserable, I started to wonder if I died. Oscar Wilde once said, "When Americans die, they go to Paris." Did this mean I was going to spend all of eternity in Paris without a lousy franc?

Suddenly I had one of those light bulb moments. I would ask everyone on the plane for a small contribution to sustain me. Gaining my courage, I stood up, announced my plight to the group, and walked down the aisle collecting funds from my kindhearted flight mates.

By the time we deplaned, my headache had cured itself, and I had enough to feed myself at least. I don't remember much more about the dream except that I was immensely happy with very little in Paris. I enjoyed the simplicity of existing on inexpensive meals and exploring every free venue in the city.

My three takeaways from my dream flight to Paris go like this:

1) Stop looking for perfection. We screw up. If you need help, ask for it. Don't try to go it alone. Sure, I had to swallow my pride and look like a blond bird-brain who doesn't have it all together, but such is life. It happens, deal with it.

2) Make the most of the moment. Whether it's a trip to Paris or your kid's soccer game, be mindful of where you are. No thinking about the mounds of unfinished work at the office or pile of laundry at home.

3) My mantra is, "There is always a Plan B." If Plan A failed, stay with your problem until you have a viable Plan B. Get creative and find a solution.

Wishing you sweet and insightful dreams!

# Time to Lower the Bar

WHILE FLIPPING THROUGH ONE OF my favorite foodie magazines, I noticed this tip: "Lower the bar. Try a no-prep picnic dinner with hard-boiled eggs, hummus, pita, olives, snap peas, and grapes." That picnic menu is appealing, but what commanded my attention was the sentence suggesting we "lower the bar." I find that phrase counter-intuitive. After all, don't we all want to create something perfectly amazing? Strange to know a chef somewhere on the planet suggests we keep it simple and stop trying so hard.

After spending a few minutes massaging that concept into my brain, I recalled a recent dinner at a friend's home. She served us a hearty but simple meal of chicken chili and cornbread. On the way home, my husband raved about the dinner. When I asked him what was so appealing, he informed me he enjoyed the simplicity of a no-fuss meal. I knew he mentally compared it to one of my "company's coming menus," which were typically rather complicated. I sighed, thinking Chef Anonymous was right about lowering the bar.

The food tip converts to a life lesson. We don't always have to create the whole enchilada. Recently a friend skilled at producing incredible cakes decided to buy one for a child's birthday party. She reasoned by keeping it simple; she could spend less time in the kitchen and more time with her guests.

There are multiple applications where it is prudent to lower the bar. If you're dreaming of that sexy, high-performance rather pricey Lexus LC 500 sports car, but you know it will be the next century before you can save enough to purchase one, take it down a few notches. It is possible to fall in love with a less expensive, lower maintenance model.

Some friends of mine put off getting married until they could afford an exquisite destination wedding. I suggested they were missing the point about celebrating a marriage, acknowledging that often guests mail in an RSVP regrets because time and travel expenses prohibit their attendance. After having some candid conversations with their friends and family, the couple found it accurate and happily tied the knot in a local venue.

What about you? Are you overly concerned about perfection? Should you lower the bar and give yourself some breathing space? Think about altering your plans.

As for me, I'm embracing, "easy" is best. Forget the pan-seared rib-eye steak with Béarnaise. Tonight the menu is chicken chili and cornbread.

# A Friendly Intervention

IF YOU NEED A REALITY check, I offer you some sage advice. Hang out with your very best friends. Select the individuals who take honesty just shy of the brutal level. Recently I experienced some cold hard truths, which I needed to hear.

Discovering I was trying too hard was a real eye-opener. Sure, I've written and coached on the dangers of reaching for perfectionism, never realizing I was careening down that slippery slope until Irma, Carol and Joan set me straight. It was high time for the coach to get some coaching, and I listened-up and soaked it all in. Letting your vulnerabilities show with people who love you is safe. There are no hidden agendas because friends don't let friends stray into dangerous territory.

Striving to achieve perfectionism is not only exhausting; it borders on obsession. Lately, a silent mantra continually drummed in my head, telegraphing the subliminal message: "Make it better." Yep, whether I was writing an article or applying my eye make-up, the results never seemed good enough. Author Anne Lamott nailed it when she said, "Perfectionism is the voice of the oppressor."

Since I've returned from the "perfectionism intervention" performed by my BFF's, I find myself laughing more and stressing less. Making the behavioral adjustment wasn't so hard. Read on as I share a few hints on how to overcome a faultfinding binge.

Begin with a little self-deprecating humor. Write down five of your imperfections and find ways to poke fun at these flaws in public over the next few days. Others appreciate your honesty. Admitting your faults makes you more authentic and likable. So fess up and share the laugher.

Another strategy I find uplifting is searching for the beauty in things that are less than perfect. For example, stop putting off something until that elusive magic moment. Rarely does the ideal time surface. Take that dress out of your closet. You know the one you've been refusing to wear until you lose five pounds. Put it on, smile and strut your stuff.

Setting time limits is a very liberating tactic. For example, are you guilty of continually reworking assignments and work presentations? In the future, set a hard stop. Give yourself one hour to do an excellent job then call it a wrap. Just focus on that four-letter word STOP and permit yourself to move on to the next activity on your list.

Always do your best, but experience peace in understanding perfection is elusive.

One last thought to remember; we all get by with a little help from our friends.

# Present Over Perfect

A FRIEND OF MINE SENT me a self-help book she claimed spoke to her on multiple levels. I read chapter after chapter in which the author, writer, speaker, wife, and mother of two worked on remaking her overly hectic life after experiencing mega burnout. Although I had empathy for the author, I didn't relate to her situation as I took in her story. About three-quarters of the way through the book, I found a chapter aimed directly at me. Yes, this one had my name on it. My author-guide talked about her incessant desire for perfection as she planned a holiday party. She knew it looked much better in her mind's eye than in reality. After much soul searching, the writer concluded she must choose "present over perfect."

Sentences like, "perfect has become as near a dirty word to me as hustle, prove, earn, complete and push," made sense. It all came to a crashing crescendo when the author wrote, "Perfect and the hunt for it will ruin our lives." Okay, I give up. Color me guilty of trying to create the perfect this, or the ideal that, and continually disappointing myself. Reading on, I got some advice on how to turn my quest for perfection on its ear.

When the author professed, "It's all about learning to show up and let ourselves be seen as we really are," I thought, wait a minute. If that means leaving the house without make-up, forget it. That's not going to happen unless it's 3:00 am, and the house is on fire.

Knowing I had to start somewhere, I chose entertaining. We invited another couple over for Saturday night dinner and drinks. Aha! Instead of scouring recipe books to design the perfect menu, I opted for a rustic Italian dish created in the slow cooker. I blew the lights out on dessert. Finding a cool creation on Pinterest involving store-bought ice cream sandwiches and whipped cream, I put it together in under seven minutes.

When I served dessert, it looked like something a 3$^{rd}$ grader cooked up. But guess what? I didn't care. It provided my guests with fits of laughter in addition to some delicious bites.

So cheers to "present over perfect." I'm getting there. If you can relate to any of this, let me know, and I'll send you the recipe.

# Baby Steps Yield
# Adult Results

THE OTHER DAY AT A board meeting, I silently observed the behavior of one of the members. Let's call her Courtney. She is someone I rather admire for her no-nonsense style. Ms. Board Lady is an individual unafraid to take a less than popular stance. Right or wrong, Courtney is rarely neutral. She voices her opinion loud and clear, never pausing to sugar-coat or dance around her point-of-view.

Although I do not always feel Courtney is right and would not want to emulate her behavior consistently, there is much to be said for people boldly generating a wave or two. Many of us hold back, terrified of making mistakes and being judged by friends and associates. Do you sometimes fall into that category? Okay, full disclosure, me too.

Some of us suffer from perfectionist tendencies. Thinking you must get it perfect is not only stifling and stressful but also impossible. In her book, *Never Good Enough: Freeing Yourself from Chains of Perfectionism*, Monica Ramirez Basco, Ph.D. warns setting high standards and working hard toward achieving those goals is not the problem. Issues occur when failing to achieve perfectionism catapults us into a whirlwind of emotional wear and tear, eventually resulting in a state of unhappiness.

Releasing our tendencies to strive for constant perfection requires a concerted effort. Martha Beck, a sociologist and renowned life coach, suggests we begin by rejecting our inner critic. You can easily recognize that demon. It is the loud voice inside your head berating you when your actions are less than flawless. Next time you pick up on that hostile inner dialect trying to prevent you from speaking up and taking action, mentally change the channel. Your inner gremlin cannot win if you refuse to play the game.

Ready to implement change? Make a pact with yourself to start pushing some boundaries. You may have to start small, but baby steps generate momentum. Remind yourself continually playing it safe is exhausting and drains you of your power. Granted, taking a stand involves a certain amount of courage and moxie, but avoiding those out-of-the-comfort-zone actions serve to keep you warming the bench.

I encourage you to break a few of your rigid rules. Get in the game, allow yourself to get down in the dirt, and get your shoes a little scruffy. Take your power back, create a few waves, and make your voice heard. So what if your actions don't measure up to your perfectionist standards. You will still win by using failure as a stepping-stone to build on.

# And the Beat Goes On

As I TUNED INTO "THE Voice," the popular American singing competition, I witnessed a contestant experiencing a timing issue. Immediately I felt his pain. Performing live in front of millions of viewers demands precision. Drawing on his courage and skill, he quickly recovered, and the remainder of the performance was flawless.

In an interview after the song, the singer admitted he came in two beats too soon on the introduction and had to start over. The judges rallied to his support, explaining that seasoned professionals mess up even after years of performing. It was at this point where the scenario went awry. Kudos to the judges for signaling forgiveness, but our wanna-be star appeared closed off to the input. He was probably experiencing a mental beating from his inner voice. Instead of relaxing into the supportive feedback, the contestant crossed his arms tightly over his chest, half-listening with pain written across his face, seemingly paralyzed by his fear of failure. I understood his disappointment but wished he had gracefully held his head high and let it go.

When are we ever going to learn, there is no such thing as perfection? Sure, it's admirable to set high standards. I support shooting for the stars, going for the gold, or striving to capture a coveted title. Conversely, we must acknowledge in the real world, not our make-believe version; professionals make errors. How many times have we witnessed star Olympic figure skaters, like Sarah Hughes or Kristi Yamaguchi landing on their backsides? Years ago, we watched "The Agony of Defeat" clip on ABC's Wild World of Sports. The producers of that show reminded the viewing audience that "the thrill of victory" is linked to defeat. Hard as we try, we don't win them all.

Many of us struggle with the obsession to never be less than picture-perfect. That is precisely an exacting term: obsession. If you find yourself in that category, it's time to make a change. I love the phrase "recovering perfectionist" because ridding yourself of the fear of one false move is a process. Begin by acknowledging that you are not your mistakes. Most importantly, committing an error is proof you are trying.

Give it your best, but realize, sometimes your best needs some rework. The next time your major presentation, job interview, or big date doesn't go as planned, spend a short moment acknowledging what went wrong and how you can improve, then move on. The test of a real winner is the ability to admit defeat graciously and the power to release, not fixate on the loss.

# Perfection

IN SUMMARY:

* Laugh at your imperfections
* Set a hard stop
* Accept supportive feedback
* No fixating on loss
* Reject your inner critic
* Push some boundaries
* Build on failure
* Ask for help
* Be seen as you are
* Present over perfect
* Allow yourself breathing space
* Best effort is enough

# Happiness
# Enjoy The Journey

"Happiness cannot be traveled to, owned, earned, worn or consumed. Happiness is the spiritual experience of living every minute with love, grace and gratitude."

— DENIS WAITLEY

# And She Called
# Me Sunny

MY CLOSE FRIENDS REFER TO me as a happiness junkie. I adore
and collect books and blogs on the subject. My favorite, *The
Happiness Project*, is a self-help memoir by Gretchen Rubin, an
author who spent twelve months methodically improving her
happiness quotient in various areas of her life. Recently I added
to my collection by downloading a bestseller by Dan Harris: *10%
Happier: How I Tamed the Voice in My Head, Reduced Stress Without
Losing My Edge, and Found Self Help That Actually Works.*

Dan's formula for creating his newfound nirvana is meditation. I confess, drawing myself into a meditative state is a highly
touted technique that eludes me. Although I absolutely suck at
sitting cross-legged on the floor, counting my breaths, and making my thoughts go away, millions succeed at this technique to
reduce stress and create a sense of calm.

Although meditation is not my forte, I am good at being
happy. Perhaps my aptitude for happiness was passed down
from my mother. When I close my eyes, I can visualize her spar-
kling blue eyes and a pair of dimples adding an extra dollop of
sunshine to the perpetual smile that graced her face. Born to

impoverished Polish immigrants, I think we can safely deduct it wasn't a wealthy upbringing that created her ever-present dazzling smile.

Mom was just naturally happy. She created a light-hearted environment for herself and others by always finding a sliver of sunshine, even in the darkest days. If something was troubling her, walking it off was her "go-to" remedy. She never owned or desired a driver's license. If a destination was beyond where her legs could carry her, she happily hopped a bus and often made friends with the driver.

My given name is Janice, but my mother sometimes called me Sunny. A sage tactic on her part, especially during my testy teenage years. Think about it. If you label your teen "a pain in the neck," she has little motivation to be anything else. Living up to a moniker like Sunny was sometimes a tall order, but perhaps Mom cracked the code with this name thing. We tell our children they are smart, so they will gain self-confidence and believe it. If you call a child by a name that reflects bright light, you continually remind her to shine.

Here's some good news: recent studies conducted at John Hopkins University School of Medicine concluded that individuals with a positive attitude are less likely to suffer a heart attack. Although I wholeheartedly support Dan Harris in his quest to master meditation and induce happiness, as for my 10%, just call me Sunny. It seems to work.

# How to Ace Happiness

IT HAPPENED AGAIN YESTERDAY. WHILE doing some volunteer work at a conference, I met Coach Valerie Alexander selling her book, *Happiness...As a Second Language*. One glance at the cover hooked me. As I rummaged through my purse for cash, Valerie presented me with a bright lemon-yellow motivational wristband declaring, "Speak Happiness." I offered up my most gracious smile. In my book, an inspirational band beats a gold bangle.

As you may already know, I am a happiness junkie. Whenever I find myself near a book about happiness, I must take it home and add it to my library. Of course, I know how to practice joy and bliss. On most days, that comes naturally. But I delight in studying happiness and aspire to one day earn an honorary degree in the subject.

As a career coach, it is sometimes my responsibility to guide clients back on the path to their happy zone. When pain and discord struts into our lives like uninvited guests, feelings of discontent take hold. Gloomy days morph into dark nights, and unless we make a concerted effort to get back to the light, depression evolves. Mood disorders gone unchecked can also influence chronic health conditions. Conversely, happiness strongly links to good health; thus, the popular cliché, "laughter is the best medicine."

In her book, Alexander writes about achieving permanent happiness. I'm not confident we can always obtain an everlasting buoyant frame of mind, but I do believe a solid understanding of techniques that negate our blue moods is our ticket to the happiness train.

So when we are stuck in reverse, what are some things that pull us out of the doldrums? My first go-to is to focus on finding one positive in a negative situation. Come on; there is always one. Stay with it until you can find it. Okay, are you feeling a bit better? Next, shift to something that needs your attention. Glimmers of happiness return when we get productive, and our troubles shift to the back burner.

When time permits, get on the move. Kick those endorphins into gear with a solid workout. Or, immerse yourself in nature. Head out the door with a notepad and jot down or photograph any sign of surrounding beauty. Want an activity more energizing? Blast the music and hold a dance party for one to your favorite playlist.

This week invest some time into understanding how to create and cultivate a positive mindset. Get serious about the study of happiness. I guarantee it's worth doing your homework on the subject. Happiness is free. And it's yours for the taking.

# Ice Cream and Cold Pizza

THE OTHER DAY I CREATED this post on social media. "You are an adult to your inner child. Permit yourself to eat ice cream for breakfast in your cowgirl boots." Judging by the likes and comments, this little ditty delighted many friends. Like me, they probably sometimes tire of being an adult. Not only is it hard work, as grown-ups, we sometimes lack the creativity and spontaneity of the young.

Are you too wound up in the parameters of adulthood? I know I am much of the time. When I need to step back, turn off the world's noise, and shake off my Ms. Manners persona, I turn to my old friend Dr. Seuss. I think he nailed it when he said, "I like nonsense. It wakes up the brain."

I always cherish reading to children by delivering the sing-song verses written by Theodore Geisel, the real name of the man dubbed as the modern Mother Goose. We loved his characters because they embraced coloring outside the lines and rarely played by the rules. (Actually, Theodore was prone to breaking the rules too, as evidenced by some trouble he got into at Dartmouth. Along with some buddies, he was caught drinking in his dorm room. I know, no big deal, right? Well, this was 1924 when prohibition reined, so there was a penalty.)

Embracing our freedom to temporarily ditch adulthood and act a bit silly means sometimes looking at the world wearing glasses two prescriptions too strong. Perhaps Seuss was doing this when he wrote: "From here to there, and there to here, funny things are everywhere."

Ready to jump on the bandwagon today and plan something fun? Break out of the permanent mold of proper grown-up behavior. Head to the mall and buy some light-up shoes to wear to work on casual Friday. Hide a bottle of soap bubbles in your desk drawer and blow them over your cube when the boss isn't looking. Get creative and mix it up a bit. As Seuss reminded us, "There is fun to be done! There are points to be scored. There are games to be won."

About breakfast, forget your morning Starbucks ritual of a non-fat decaf cappuccino or your skinny green tea latte. Stop at the nearest Ben and Jerry's and opt for a scoop of one of their insane flavors like Coconuts for Caramel. As for me, I might show up at the breakfast table wearing a pink tutu and munching on cold pizza, my favorite wacky breakfast treat.

# It's The Little Things

I've been preparing for a big move for weeks. Yes, I'm trading in life in the Golden State for my next chapter in the Sunshine State. If you've ever moved across the country or across the street, you know that there are many decisions to be made when it comes to your personal belongings. For me, the big stuff is a cakewalk. Selling my furniture, and giving away clothing, kitchenware, and electronics, all a no-brainer. It's the little things that give me pause. Articles like a mug, a shawl, a tray, a Christmas ornament, a selection of unusual spices, all gifted to me by friends, will not be left behind.

That's the way it is in life, right? The pint-sized items or happenings make your heart sing and bring you joy. A mother's smile, a first kiss, the smell of coffee brewing in the morning, your fourth grader's first home run, the list is infinite. It might be Pooh who said, "Sometimes the smallest things take up the most room in your heart." Well said, dear Pooh. And for all of life's little things, we should express gratitude.

We can also view this "little thing" concept from a goal achievement perspective. Scoring small wins count when working toward the big goal. As Van Gogh stated, "Great things are done by a series of small things brought together." He certainly proved it with each tiny little brushstroke.

Sometimes something small inadvertently turns into a significant accomplishment. I once read that Dale Carnegie's mega-best-seller, *How to Win Friends and Influence People,* started with a short speech that expanded to a workshop, soon after became a course and eventually, the book. According to Wikipedia, over 15 million copies of this book have been sold worldwide. So maybe the life lesson here is, dream big but start small. Consider the possibility of something you start as a little project.

So my advice is twofold. Take notice of and delight in the little things. Show appreciation to the guy who let you cut into traffic, the barista who made you the perfect Tall Flat White, and the sound of your loved one's laughter. At the same time, review your catalog of mini projects and determine if you've created a diamond in the rough. The possibilities are endless.

# Once Upon a Time

DURING A COACHING SESSION, A client remarked she was on a mission to find her "inner child." Her words inspired me. I never really thought much about the subject, so I did some research.

Of course, we have an inner child because once upon a time, we were children. Who is this little person of your inner being? Answer: your inner child is the fun-loving, happy, frivolous, joyful, humorous you. It's the "you" before you changed into the sophisticated, mature, solemn, and task-oriented you of today. Remember the younger you? Can you recall when the only serious decision you made was which one of the 31 flavors to select at the local Baskin Robbins?

Experts say we should embrace our inner child. Even the brilliant Albert Einstein quipped, "Play is the highest form of research." As adults, we obsess over little things. Kids are carefree. They do whatever they enjoy. Children neither jam their calendars with meaningless events because it's expected nor obsess over calories or go nuts if the house isn't spotless. What they do is laugh, a lot. I mean indulge in big-time laughter, not just little giggles. Children roll on the floor, letting out loud belly laughs. According to information released from the Mayo Clinic, hearty laughter reduces stress by stimulating circulation and helping muscle relaxation. No wonder kids lead a stress-free life.

When it comes to activities, kids are master event planners. Ask a child what they like to do and you will get bombarded with seventy-nine trillion fun-filled ideas. For example, children love picnics. They don't mind ants (some are known to eat them), and they are okay with getting dirty. The best thing about kids is they know how to play. It's spontaneous with them. Kids do not have to anchor it into an activity list. Ever watch a child at play? It's exhausting! Children whirl and dig and zoom and jump. They tumble and skip and hop and twirl. Kids are experts at squeezing every ounce of fun out of their day.

With a little help from Professor Einstein and data from the Mayo Clinic, I see the benefits of finding my inner child. As of today, I am resolving to spend more time with people under the age of five. I desire to be a person who knows how to have fun and play. I'm going to lighten up, laugh more, and not take myself so seriously. Are you with me? As a wise person once said, "Play is not a luxury; it's a necessity."

# Would You Rather Be a Fish?

LAST EVENING I HAD A conversation with my five-year-old niece Alina. We discussed all things Thanksgiving: her mom's famous lumpy gravy, which she pretends to like, her nana's yummy pumpkin mousse, requiring no acting, and the games she intends to play with visiting cousins. As the conversation progressed, I asked her what one thing topped her thankful list. Without missing a beat, she said her swim class. I inquired why this was such a monumental blessing. Alina sighed as if I didn't get it and patiently explained that when she gets in the water, she is no longer Alina, the girl, she becomes Alina the fish. She continued her monologue by relating as a fish she could race with the other fish, open her eyes underwater, and she didn't have to go to school. When I informed her that fish swim in schools, she laughed, called me a silly auntie, and said goodnight.

As I whispered up a prayer that night, I gave thanks both for Alina, the girl, and Alina, the fish. I found it interesting that I struck her as silly because it suddenly occurred to me lately; my life was lacking in the laughter department. Making a vow to be more like Alina, fun, and carefree, I drifted off to sleep.

Yep, adulting is tough stuff. Getting caught up in a myriad of activities, especially around hectic holiday seasons, finds many of us complaining we are crazy busy. Giving in to this busyness and letting it take control drives us to lose connection with the joyful, creative child of our youth.

In her book, *Recovery of Your Inner Child,* Dr. Lucia Capacchione explains we each possess a "playful child" who has a real capacity for joy. This inner child emerges when you delight in playing with your dog, hiking a nature trail, or even singing in the shower.

If you feel your zest for life waning, it may be time to reconnect with your playful side. Take a moment to clear away some of the busyness from your calendar. Replace those mundane duties with activities that bring joy. Go to the zoo, take your dog to the park or watch a funny flick. Take a trip to a hobby shop, read a children's book, and give yourself permission to skip. And don't forget to walk in the rain. A wise person once said, "A man is getting old when he walks around a puddle instead of through it."

As for me, I'm off to one of those "build a bear" shops. Want to join me? We'll bring out the inner child in both of us.

# ACKNOWLEDGMENTS

"Feeling gratitude and not expressing it is like
wrapping a present and not giving it."

— WILLIAM ARTHUR WARD

Yes, Mr. Ward, I agree. And now it's my turn to offer up gratitude to the incredible people who inspired and supported me along the way. So, in no particular order, I would like to thank the following individuals.

Sincere appreciation to my writing mentors, Judith Fabris, and Ellen Paris. Both have helped me become a better writer throughout the years. Extra special gratitude to Judith for writing the forward, and to Ellen for talking me off the ledge when I faced the fear of getting my words out into the world.

Additionally, many thanks to Dixie Angelo and Linsey Moore-Vandenbos, the amazing members of our critique group.

Gratitude to my forever friends. Without your inspiration, love, and encouragement, there would be no book. You know who you are; you find yourself in the pages of *Life on the Sunny Side*.

Thanks to Jen Altieri of Hope Inrheart Life Coaching for inviting me to her motivational Vision Board Workshop. She set the stage for making the book a 2020 reality.

I am grateful to Jay Stringer for lending his marketing expertise.

To my nieces, Aisalynn and Alina, who taught me essential lessons during each step of their development, I am forever grateful.

Thanks to Tracy Dietlin and Phil Lacombe of The Coachella Valley Weekly for the opportunity to write for their publication and hone my craft.

Sincere appreciation to my team Durski, and Tracie Schatz, for all their hard work in getting this publication to press.

Love and gratitude to my wonderful husband, John, who always believes in me and champions my life work.

Thank you to God for giving me the passion to share my stories in this book and the tenacity and grace to see it through.

# ABOUT THE AUTHOR

Sunny Simon hails from the Midwest where she earned her Bachelor's degree at Central Michigan University. Typical of her nickname, "Sunny" fled the cold climate seeking a place in the sun. Since then, she has resided in both Florida and California.

Prior to becoming a writer and life and career coach, Sunny spent twenty years in the field of human resources. It offered everything she loved, the opportunity to be a talent scout, a compensation guru, and a consultant to management. During her corporate career, she worked for both Fortune 500 companies and start-ups in Silicon Valley.

Known as an incurable optimist and master change agent, she is passionate about writing. In addition to her coaching business, she wrote a weekly column doling out life and career advice in the "CV Weekly," a regional publication in California's Coachella Valley.

After years in both northern and southern California, Sunny and husband John returned to balmy south Florida. Happily settled into a cozy condo across the street from the ocean, she is free to pursue her passion for writing. She affectionately labels this new adventure "Florida 2.0"

When not writing or spurring a client on to their next big challenge, you will find her enjoying sunrise walks on the beach and leisurely savoring just caught freshly grilled fish at funky ocean side cafes.

More about Sunny at www.raisethebarhigh.com

Made in the USA
Columbia, SC
27 October 2020

23610664R00231